Partnerships in Education Research

Partnerships in Education Research

Creating Knowledge that Matters

MICHAEL ANDERSON AND KELLY FREEBODY

B L O O M S B U R Y

LONDON • NEW DELHI • NEW YORK • SYDNEY

Bloomsbury Academic

An imprint of Bloomsbury Publishing Plc

50 Bedford Square	1385 Broadway
London	New York
WC1B 3DP	NY 10018
UK	USA

www.bloomsbury.com

Bloomsbury is a registered trade mark of Bloomsbury Publishing Plc

First published 2014

British Library Cataloguing-in-Publication Data
A catalogue record for this book is available from the British Library.

ISBN: HB: 978-1-4411-1115-9
PB: 978-1-4411-5898-7
ePDF: 978-1-4411-3411-0
ePub: 978-1-4411-9553-1

Library of Congress Cataloging-in-Publication Data
Anderson, Michael, 1969-
Partnerships in education research : creating knowledge that matters / Michael Anderson and Kelly Freebody.
pages cm
Includes bibliographical references and index.
ISBN 978-1-4411-1115-9 (hardback)—ISBN 978-1-4411-5898-7 (pbk.)—
ISBN 978-1-4411-3411-0 (epdf)—ISBN 978-1-4411-9553-1 (epub)
1. Education—Research. 2. Research teams. I. Freebody, Kelly. II. Title.
LB1028.A477 2014
370.72—dc23
2013033735

Typeset by RefineCatch Limited, Bungay, Suffolk
Printed and bound in Great Britain

CONTENTS

LIST OF FIGURES AND TABLES

Figures

Tables

Boxes

PREFACE

Partnerships in Education Research: Creating Knowledge that Matters
examines methodological and logistical issues that researchers face when
conducting partnership research in teams. Research partnerships are now
prevalent in universities and industry with a large proportion of public and
private research funds being devoted to collaborations between government,
non-government and industry organizations and this book is intended to
honour and support the growth of partnership research.

Despite its prevalence, partnership research can be challenging to
manage in supportive, productive and sustainable ways. This book is
designed to be a starting point for those looking for guidance in this
potentially difficult area of research. It is not intended as a cookbook or a
set of checklists (although we do provide some principles along the way) for
researchers to get right, but rather as an attempt to consider how we manage
partnership research to 'make knowledge matter'. It discusses partnership
research from a researcher's perspective (through case studies) and provides
examples of methodologies that can be applied to partnership research. This
book will be relevant for researchers seeking to attract, develop and sustain
research partnerships. Even though it is in large part written for the
researcher, the book does also provide support for those in industry, NGO,
philanthropic or public sector organizations seeking to undertake partnership
research.

We have tried as far as possible to provide examples of partnership
research that reflect the arguments we are making in these chapters. Some of
the projects we present in the case studies emerge from our own practice,
while other projects we have become aware of as exemplars of partnership
research.

The book focuses on two main forms of partnership research: Academic-
led research supported by an industry partner (such as the Economic and
Social Research Council grant programs and the Australian Research
Council Linkage grants) and practice-led research supported or facilitated
by a critical friend such as action research in schools, supervising the work
of research students, and facilitating design-based research interventions.
These two common forms of partnership research require different levels of
engagement, critique and management (intellectual and practical) from
partners and often support different methodologies, practices and theoretical
foundations. We explore these issues in the chapters of this book.

The book has two main guiding themes. Firstly we explore the epistemological and philosophical basis for engaging with partners in research. Through this we discuss theoretical, ethical and socio-cultural aspects of partnership research and the potential for partnership research to have long lasting effects on industry/NGO practice. Secondly, this book is concerned with practise, providing illustrative examples (case studies) of effective partnership research from education with links to medicine, law, the arts, social work and sociology). These case studies are drawn from North America, South East Asia and Australasia to provide a sense what is possible in many parts of the world. *Partnerships in Education Research* concludes with a series of principles and models that can be applied to the development of an effective partnership research project.

There are many research stories and we have only presented a tiny fraction of the stories of partnership research. Our hope is that we, through writing this book, can make a small contribution to the further growth of partnership research. We would like to provide some encouragement for partnership researchers working in education to face and overcome their challenges and to enjoy the satisfaction gained from partnership research. Hopefully through this process many more stories of successful partnership research will emerge.

ACKNOWLEDGEMENTS

We would like to thank all the partners, in schools and in various industries we have worked with over our careers. With you we have learned so much, not only about education, but about research and research processes.

We would like to acknowledge the generosity of colleagues whose work we've used as exemplars in this volume – not only do you do great, innovative work, but you are generous with your knowledge. Specifically, we'd like to thank George Belliveau, Deb Hayes, Peter O'Connor, Christine Sinclair and Madonna Stinson.

Thank you to our editor Alison Baker, Rosie Pattinson, Frances Arnold and all the staff at Bloomsbury for their patience and hard work in the editorial process.

Finally, we'd like to thank our families – Henry, Tom, Harriet, Rebecca and Ewan. For their love and support, and for never complaining about how often they ended up eating take away during the writing of this book.

Michael and Kelly

CHAPTER ONE

Making knowledge matter

Most of us who work in education as teachers, researchers or both do so because we value the relationships that are at the heart of learning and teaching. At its core, learning and teaching involve a series of relationships; teacher to student, teacher to teacher, student to student and so on. Essentially, then, good teaching and learning is dependent upon effective relationships. How teachers relate to students, how students relate to the curriculum or how school leaders relate to the community. It follows then that researchers must establish solid and sustainable partnerships to create, design and deliver effective research.

This book in general, and this chapter in particular, is devoted to the relationships that are at the heart of educational research. In this opening chapter we will provide a rationale for doing research in partnerships and define various partnerships available to researchers and professionals in educational settings. We also set out some of the qualities of effective partnerships and discuss the politics, challenges and benefits of partnership research. Finally, we consider how educators and researchers can create a mutually beneficial relationship to deliver high quality research. This chapter outlines the rationale underpinning partnership research and our commitment as educational researchers to make knowledge matter to students, teachers, policymakers and the community.

Partnership research is not new, most if not all research is done in a partnership of one kind or another such as a funding body, an organization or the research participants. The history of research in the social sciences and in education particularly is marked by the emergence of practitioner-based research such as participatory action-based research and design based research (Carr and Kemmis 2003; Reimann 2011). The emergence and prevalence of these methodologies in education signifies the centrality of praxis; the notion that knowledge creation in education is informed by both theory and practice (Freire 1972). The nature and complexity of the relationships in educational research influence how and why we undertake partnership research in education. The ideas in this book align with approaches to research that incorporate notions of praxis including practitioner-led methodologies, arts-informed practice and other methods that address the multi-layered nature of educational practice.

Making knowledge matter in education

One of the reasons we chose to situate the discussions in this book around education is because schools and school systems are very particular places to conduct research. While 'particular' is a fairly neutral word, let's begin with a focus on the good news about why schools are great places in which to do research. Education practitioners are unique in their position to effect change.

Educators are often key figures in the communities in which they work; they have access to a cross section of the community, including local businesses, government agencies, parents, and young people. Educators are also responsible for interpreting and implementing policy, often large 'one size fits all' ideas, for and in their local environments in ways that are supposed to meet the needs of local communities (Freebody, P., Freebody, K. and Maney 2011a). Therefore researchers in education have a uniquely exponential ability to make knowledge matter because they work directly with school leaders, teachers and students who are at the forefront of applying policy in diverse communities. In a very real sense, the new knowledge and understanding created by research in education can change the way young people are taught, the way teachers engage in professional development, the way curriculums are planned and the way schools engage with their local communities.

This does not mean that research in education is without its challenges. Schools are notoriously busy places; often overpopulated with policies, sometimes full of conflicting ideas, purpose and procedure, almost always weighed down by multiple layers of bureaucracy and often staffed with overworked, time-poor teachers. To many, the complex nature of education and schooling seems daunting. One of the key ideas in this book is that those working in partnership research in education need to be, not just aware of, but engaged with the various stakeholders and 'layers' of the system. For new knowledge and ideas to matter in education, they must have practical and theoretical significance for a range of levels in the system, including:

- the teachers and students in the classroom;
- the leadership of schools – principals, deputies, deans of studies, welfare officers;
- the parents and communities served by the school/s;

- regional systems – depending on the context of the research. This may include regional literacy coordinators, department officers, dioceses, local government;

- state or national systems – including policy and curriculum development; and

- the academic community who is responsible for disseminating the research findings and training the next generation of teachers.

While all working in the same system, and seemingly all for the good of the same students, these different layers of education respond to their own local concerns and needs, which are sometimes quite removed from (or indeed, in contrast to) the layers around them (Cheng and Tam 1997). These layers do, however, rely quite heavily on each other to get the everyday business of school done. Curriculums and policies are written by state/national systems and then interpreted by regional officers who provide professional development for schools. Principals then interpret the local meaning of these policies in their school plans and teachers programme for their particular classes using information from the national policies/curriculums, the regional input, the whole school plan and their own interpretation of all of the above. School leaders, teachers and students then interpret these policies, plans and curriculums for the wider community, including parents. Even this complicated paragraph over-simplifies the kind of work that happens in schools – actually there's also probably input from local clubs, theatres, sports groups, or churches; government interagencies with a presence in the school; connections with universities including training student teachers; there might be counsellors or speech pathologists that the teachers also work with; and of course the teachers work with each other, sharing resources and plans. Throw in a few research projects and researchers and . . . as we said before, schools are busy and complex places.

Not only are they busy but also education systems in general are difficult places to implement policy change. In discussions about school reform Elmore refers to three 'conceits' or 'fallacies' typically embodied by education policy (Elmore 1996: p. 499):

1 *The newest policy takes precedence over all previous policies*, whereas, in reality the effect is usually more additive – new policies are added to an already crowded and complex policy environment in schools where they often sit uncomfortably, potentially confusing or contradicting existing policies and practices.

2 *Policies originate from one level of the education system and 'embody a single message about what schools should do differently'* (Elmore 1996: p. 499), whereas, in reality a policy or reform may be initiated in one part of the system, but the interconnectedness of education practice means that these policies become layered as other parts of the

system engage with the development of the policy. For example, in Australia, a policy regarding school literacy improvement does not just concern state literacy consultants, it also requires input from parts of the system that work with disadvantaged schools, Aboriginal education, teacher training and professional development, education budget managers, politicians, community liaison officers, the list goes on. Not only do these sections of the system have different foci, but they sometimes have competing ideas about why, how and for whom policies should be implemented.

3   *That policies operate in the same way no matter what setting they are implemented*, whereas, as we have discussed, policies reach the classroom after being filtered through a variety of contexts and systems. As a result, they are put into everyday classroom practice in a variety of ways, for a variety of purposes that are specific to the local site's interpretation of the policy and needs more generally.

These three 'conceits' are pertinent to our discussions of how we make research in education matter for a range of reasons. We chose to outline them here, however, for two main reasons. Firstly while many people acknowledge that working in a school is complex, we wanted to specifically draw attention to the complexity of education policy and reform – as much of the research done in education aims to effect or develop these two areas. Researchers should be sceptical of the extent to which a 'one size fits all' policy or reform, dictated from a capital city office building, can effect real change in classrooms. This is not to say we do not need reform or that it should not come from central offices. We need to be aware of the potential impact our research has on the education communities we are researching with. Secondly, we want to make the more positive and productive point that by working in partnership with education (and organizations on the periphery of education) we can make powerful change in a complex education system. Essentially, our argument in this book is that partnership research in education is crucial because, if it successfully navigates the borders and layers of the system, it can create knowledge that actually ends up mattering on the everyday level of the classroom as well as the macro and meso levels of the school and system.

Partnership research is. . .

Pretty much all of our lives as researchers are lived in partnerships. When we use the term partnership research in this book we are referring to a partnership between a researcher and a research context, and the people who associate with that context. Although classically in education, partnership research occurs between researchers and teachers, it could also involve partnerships with schools, government departments, community education centres, outdoor education centres, businesses or any organization concerned with education. Our aim in this book is to challenge the subject–object conceptualization that entrenches hierarchies between 'researcher' and 'researched'. While we acknowledge there will always be hierarchies in relationships, the ultimate aim of partnership research is to recalibrate the research conversation making it more of a discussion than a monologue. The word partner is defined by the *OED* (2013) as 'the fact or condition of being a partner; association or participation; companionship', but perhaps more realistically for the research endeavour this sense of partnership as either people dancing together or playing a game or sport on the same side might be more fitting. You may have noticed already that we have avoided using words like 'subject' to describe those *with* whom we are researching. This choice of language is deliberate and signals a commitment to changing the way research is conceptualized to create space for more democratic and engaged relationships between researchers and their partners in research. This conceptualization of research harnesses the practical knowledge, skills and understanding of both the researcher and the partner recognizing that they have different but essential roles. Metaphorically, this kind of research is symbiotic rather than parasitic. There is an exchange that reflects equilibrium in the relationship. This has wide-ranging implications for the research relationship that permeate the ways we design, implement and communicate the research. This may take more time and effort than 'old paradigm' research, but we argue that this approach is a more sustainable and democratic way to work in partnership with communities to create more connected and relevant knowledge.

The scope of partnership research is quite broad and ranges from an individual teacher working in a classroom with a researcher to a large multidisciplinary research team of researchers working with schools internationally, and everything in between. We have been involved in many of these kinds of research and between us we have had the roles of researcher and partner throughout our careers. So while we write this book in our current perspectives as educational researchers we have experience in and are sensitive to the needs and requirements of the partner. When we discuss partnership research we are not necessarily referring to the process often described as collaborative research (Zittoun et al. 2007) where researchers work with each other. While much partnership is undertaken by collaborative teams this is not the focus of this book.

Who's who in partnership research?

For the sake of clarity we will refer to two main roles in partnership research. When we refer to the individual or team undertaking the research we will call them the researcher or the research team. If we are referring to schools and the individuals who are participating in the research we refer to them as the partner. This delineation is arbitrary and we acknowledge that these roles are never as clear cut as we have described them here. There is of course a danger that by defining the roles in this way we will entrench a dichotomy that is against the spirit and practice of partnership research. After all, we do want to reconceptualize partnership research as a team-based 'sport' rather than an individual quest. If we do not define the different roles, however, we risk not recognizing that partners and researchers bring different skills, expectations and experiences to research. One of the aims of exploring partnership research in this way is to be as explicit as possible about the challenges and opportunities for all in the research partnership.

A theoretical perspective on partnership research

There should, in our view, be a connection between what we aspire to in schooling and the way we research education. Therefore, a theoretical perspective of partnership research starts with an understanding of the various perspectives underpinning education practice. According to Freire, the critical educator, good practice alone will not bring about transformative education. Action only becomes productive when it is informed by beliefs, objectives, theoretical perspectives and historical understandings and is then coupled with constant reflection. In his foundational work, *Pedagogy of the Oppressed*, Freire calls for educators to engage, not just in practice, but in praxis – a combination of 'reflection and action upon the world in order to transform it' (Freire 1970: p. 36). When we discuss praxis in this book, we are referring to 'the complex combination of theory and practice, resulting in informed action' (Kincheloe 2008: p. 120).

Research in education effects and is affected by multiple perspectives and priorities including how we practice, theorize, research and make policy. As we discussed earlier, this means that for the new knowledge and understandings created by partnership research in education to matter, they need to be informed by the goals, and address the needs, of many. As a result, we believe that both research and practice need to be constantly reflective and constantly informing one another. Action precipitating reflection that precipitates further transforming action. In our opinion these ideas inform educators' (including researchers' and teachers') beliefs and objectives in undertaking partnership research and therefore make our actions more purposeful and productive.

Another central tenet shared by both education practice and partnership research is their collaborative nature. Communities of practice are present in many areas of our lives, but especially in the domains of research and schooling (Anderson and Freebody 2012). Communities of Practice approaches spring from sociocultural theory, based on the work of Vygotsky (1978). Communities of practice recognize a shift from an individualistic approach to a communal construction of practice such as learning and research (Barab et al. 2002: p. 489). Wenger defines a community of practice as a result of collective learning that

> reflects both the pursuit of our enterprises and the attendant social relations. These practices are thus the property of a kind of community created over time by the sustained pursuit of a shared enterprise. It makes sense; therefore to call these kinds of communities, communities of practice. (Wenger 1998: p. 45)

In the context of research, we argue that these co-constructed processes are in action. The collaboration between several individuals from several backgrounds, be they other researchers or partners, provides a community of praxis (Anderson and Freebody 2012) that can lead to rich discoveries about the links between theory and practice in education. In this sense partnership research 'can be considered as an activity . . . inasmuch as it is a culturally laden context where the participants learn and use specific actions and operations in order to reach their aims, established, often recursively, during the research endeavour' (Pontecorvo 2007: p. 179). Researching collaboratively with partners provides authentic insights into educational contexts that are not possible working from an outsider's perspective.

Alongside sociocultural theory there is a belief that learning should be collaborative and experiential. These ideas, in part, make up the progressive and critical education movement that has been a feature of education theory over the last century. John Dewey was an influential scholar in education and beyond. His work has been significant for teachers and researchers since the publication of *My Pedagogy Creed* (Dewey 1897). One of Dewey's concerns was for schools was to instil collaborative learning approaches. He claimed that

> it behoves the school to make ceaseless and intelligently organized effort to develop above all else the will for co-operation and the spirit which sees in every other individual one who has an equal right to share in the cultural and material fruits of collective human invention. (Dewey 1937)

Drawing on these understandings of the practice of education, researchers in the field were challenged to devise methodologies that took account of practice in the development of educational praxis. The participatory action research movement that we explore in more detail in Chapter 8 (Carr and Kemmis 2003) arose from a frustration with the binary, status ridden traditional research approaches (Creswell 1994). Commenting on the advantages of collaboration in action research, Carr and Kemmis (2003) argue that the approach offers:

a first step to overcoming aspects of the existing social order which frustrate rational change: it organizes practitioners into collaborative groups for the purposes of their own enlightenment, and in doing so, it creates a model for a rational and democratic social order. The practice of collaborative educational action research envisages a social order characterized by rational communication, just and democratic decision making, and fulfilling work. Moreover, it focuses the participants on their own educational action with the intention of reforming it so that educational practices, understandings and situations are no longer marred by contradictions or distorted by ideology. (Carr and Kemmis 2003: p. 200)

While in practice we believe action research has much to offer educational practitioners and researchers we are not comfortable with the claim that action research is or has the potential to be ideology free. Teachers and researchers are often ideologues and the 'action' that is the focus of the research is routinely based on the ideological belief that education can and should be done better. In our view ideology should not be concealed but rather made transparent, as it is often a driver for reform in educational settings.

Since the development of action research, practitioner-led research in education has become an established form of professional learning. This is a healthy sign for education as a field of practice and a site for research. It suggests that education researchers should remain connected to current practice, as it is likely to be at the centre of their research agendas. Lyn Yates argues that research in education has specific influences depending on the context and intent of the 'research players'. She says that our field is 'not simply characterized by some abstract search for knowledge but a field of practice where different players have their own sense of what is needed or desirable' (Yates 2004: p. 21). This tension between theory and practice is why there is a focus by teachers, bureaucrats and policymakers on approaches that relate to classrooms more directly. This uncovers a double bind for researchers. Universities and publishers expect research to be reported in a manner that is often not accessible for audiences outside the academic community. Part of the difficulty here is that some education researchers only seek one audience for their work when it is often directly relevant or could be beneficial for several audiences. We explore the dissemination of research in more depth in Chapter 10. What is worth understanding, at least initially, is that researchers are often doing their work for multiple audiences and the design, implementation and the dissemination of that work should recognize those multiple audiences.

The methodological 'tug o' war'

In the current climate a televised tug o' war is taking place between the public good – which requires simple questions, answers and solutions that are reportable, fundable and easily understood – and the complex, messy, busy reality of educational practice. Educational researchers need to navigate between public expectations and maintaining integrity in their research. Research decisions, particularly about methodology, are influenced by this tug o' war. Historically, educational researchers have expressed concern that the 'public' demand for simple answers has led to an increased focus on quantitative measures. We are not claiming that one approach should be favoured above the other. Rather that the methodologies respond to the variety of questions that educators need answers for. In essence, we should not be deluded into thinking that the complex questions (Barnett 2000) that arise in education can be responded to with methodologies that do not take account of that complexity. We have already alluded to one of the key issues that partnership researchers in education and practitioners face on a daily basis – complexity. A senior colleague once commented to us that the nature of education research was 'untangling the many variables to understand how educators can make a difference in the lives of their students'. He is right of course and it is a particular challenge for those working in quantitative research to untangle the complexities and distil those complexities into mainly numerical measures. On the other hand, qualitative research methods can provide researchers with the tools to incorporate these complexities in their projects. Research teams using qualitative methods can explore complexity from multiple methodological and sometimes epistemological standpoints for different audiences. The capacity to analyse and reflect complexity, however, can also lead to confusing and muddled outcomes of the research. What we are saying here, without getting into an unedifying and ultimately pointless discussion around the relative benefits of quantitative versus qualitative research, is that the methods chosen depend entirely on the intended outcomes, the research question and the research contexts. Complexity is a feature of the field that cannot be wished away (and nor should it). It is part of the educational research landscape that makes it a unique and exciting place to work.

The politics of evidence-based practice

At first glance it seems reasonable, perhaps even axiomatic that we should require evidence to make changes in practice or policy in education. A critical issue, however, *the* critical issue, is what counts as evidence and what evidence counts? Evidence-based research is a contested term in this field. Lyn Yates prefers the term 'scientifically-based' (Yates 2004: p. 24) research to avoid the issues that surround the use of the term 'evidence' and to cut to the heart of what is really meant by the term; that it is research based on empiricism. Denzin argues that there is a concerning new trend in research that privileges certain types of evidence over others:

Like an elephant in the living room, the evidence-based practice model is an intruder whose presence can no longer be ignored. Within the global audit culture, proposals concerning the use of ... experimental methodologies, randomized control trials, quantitative metrics, citation analyses shared databases, journal impact factors, rigid notions of accountability, data transparency, warrantability, rigorous peer-review evaluation scales and fixed formats for scientific articles now compete, fighting to gain ascendency in the evidence-quality-standards discourse. (Denzin 2011: pp. 11–12)

We believe that this tendency for certain types of evidence has moved beyond the academy and into the work of teachers. Some in the community, no longer trust that teachers 'know', we need evidence and metrics to demonstrate that this is the case. The autonomous decisions once the domain of teachers is increasingly centrally monitored (Nieto 2013).

This is a potential schism for that has already managed to divide many education researchers and blunt the effectiveness of the field. In our view, partnership research does not need to be divided in this way. As we have mentioned, researchers in education especially must be aware of their audiences. Building a team around each partnership project necessitates an understanding of the needs of the research partner and the eventual audiences for the research. We have used this approach on several occasions to good effect and it swiftly avoids pointless arguments between scientifically-based and other research.

There are some critical battles to be fought over what counts as evidence, and education should cherish and defend its place as a field that encourages a multitude of educational research approaches that take account of complexity. Evidence in our field should be broadly understood and we should defend the right of many approaches to be acknowledged as evidence-based. Evidence is at the core of most research. It is critical that as part of all our partnership research projects we make the arguments for why our various approaches and methodologies are 'evidence-based' and how the different methods collect different kinds of evidence to answer different kinds of questions. There should be space in educational research for a multiplicity of methods that create meaning from diverse sources of data. Relying on just one or two methodologies or epistemologies will narrow, perhaps irrevocably, what is possible in research. We will examine methodologies in more detail in Chapter 8.

Types of partnership research

To this point we have defined the partnership research relationship quite broadly, as a kind of metaphorical dance. There are however many kinds of dance styles and they suit different approaches and temperaments and come from different contexts. This introductory chapter outlines some of the common types of partnership research that will be explored in greater detail throughout the book.

- *Research Higher Degrees*
  The first experience most researchers have with partnership research is through their honours, Masters or PhD. It is here that many of the understandings about research are 'laid down' and many of the habits of partnership research are formed. In both of our PhD research projects we worked with schools to understand how teachers and students attitudes are formed and how they influence their future pathways. Working on this micro level allowed us to develop relationships and understand how partnerships work before scaling up to other kinds of partnership research.

- *Evaluation research*
  Evaluation is a common but sometimes difficult form of partnership research. The evidence-based culture has spawned a burgeoning industry for those with expertise in educational research for programme evaluation. The popularity of evaluation can be traced to the constant call for transparency in the expenditure of educational funding. While increased evaluation of programmes is on the face of it, good for the field, difficulties can arise when research is bought and there is a lack of understanding about the respective roles of the evaluators (the researcher) and the client (the partner).

- *Partner led research*
  Partner led research in education is research that is instigated by the partner; such as a teacher, school leader or youth club. It is often not payment-based but rather involves the partner approaching a researcher to work collaboratively with them on investigating issues relevant to them. For example, a teacher based in a school approaches a researcher to work with them on a small-scale issue. Recently, a colleague of ours, who is an educational researcher, was approached by a boy's high school that many people would regard as a 'challenging school'. The teacher had met her while our colleague was visiting the school as a practicum supervisor and began discussing the use of music in the maths classroom. The teacher wanted to investigate if and how learning improved across maths and music if they were taught in a more integrated way. What ensued was a small-scale piece of research that looked into this issue and made some research conclusions that changed the teacher's approach to the teaching of music and mathematics. This is an example of small-scale partner-initiated research. Much partner led research occurs in meso and macro levels of the system. For example, government departments may issue a tender for research relating to their programmes.

- *Funded projects*

Funded projects usually begin with the awarding of funds including grants, postdoctoral awards and research fellowships. By funded research we are referring to projects that are closely aligned to the researcher's interest. However, there is a growing middle ground between funded projects and projects that link researchers with partners. There is an increasing number of schemes that are encouraging researchers to engage in 'knowledge transfer' or 'linkages' with partners. In the United Kingdom the Economic and Social Research Council (ESRC) describes the object of such schemes in this way:

> At the heart of each Knowledge Transfer Partnership is a relationship between a company/organization and staff in a knowledge-based institution. The institution's staff apply their expertise to a project that will help the development of their collaborative partner. The project is carried out by an associate (a recent graduate or postgraduate), who also benefits from an organized training programme. In the process, the business relevance of the knowledge base of the institution is enhanced. (ESRC 2012)

The rhetoric of 'knowledge transfer' is something that partnership researches will notice frequently. In this ESRC scheme there is an attempt to formalize the partnership and create an interchange of ideas. As we will discuss later, this is not always 'smooth sailing' but schemes such as these do signal an intensifying interest on the behalf of funding agencies to support projects that involve partners and that appear to be applied to places like businesses and schools.

Who gets the benefits of partnerships research?

There's a simple answer to this question and a more complex answer. The simple answer is 'everyone'. If you believe, as we do, that new understandings in education can help us do our job better (and by us we mean teachers, leaders, policymakers, researchers and teacher/educators), then research in partnerships with schools and other education-focused organizations is integral to our work. To explore the more complex answer to the question, let us analyse the benefits according to the different 'stakeholders' in partnership research:

Benefits for the researchers: Researchers benefit from partnership research for a variety of reasons. A key reason is that working with partners gives researchers access to insights into how the research work is informed by, and informing, current practice. Rather than schools being merely data collection sites, working in partnership with schools transforms them to richer, research and data-informing sites allowing for an exchange of ideas. Practically, this allows researchers to develop a deeper understanding of the site and how the features of the site inform the research questions. Epistemologically, it allows for researchers to engage in praxis – connecting their work theory, research and practice in education, and therefore partnership research can also have significant benefits for theory development. When we connect the question 'how does partnership research benefit researchers' with 'how do you make research knowledge matter', another benefit emerges. When researchers work directly with education practitioners, the findings from the research have a direct influence on the practice of those working in schools. If we return to Elmore's (1996) concern that educational policy is not necessarily having enough (or the desired) effect on the everyday work in classrooms, we can see the significance of this type of work not just for the researcher and partner involved, but also how it may also *benefit policymakers*.

Benefits for the partners: Once again, we'll return to the importance of praxis in this discussion. Schools and teachers that are engaged in the development of new theories and understandings through research have the opportunities to act more deliberately and knowledgeably in their work. Being involved in partnership research, therefore, offers potential *benefits for practice*. The current evidence-based climate in education in many countries requires teachers and school leaders to engage more and more in research into their own programmes and practices (Kinchloe 2003). Schools are often called on to 'prove worth' by providing evidence of a need or a capacity. When schools apply for funding for specialist teachers, for permission to undertake specialist programmes, or for opportunities to become centres of excellence or develop interagency links with community organizations, they are often reliant on the school's or a teacher's ability to 'make the case'. Therefore there are practical benefits for educators who become involved in research – not only does much of the research directly *benefit the school* by responding to a particular need it may have – but also allows those involved to become skilled in research methodologies, vocabularies, and practices for their own use. So there are benefits for schools and other educational organizations being directly involved in research, rather than having the findings interpreted for them in a decontextualized manner through a general policy response.

Beyond the school, partnership research in education provides *benefits for the community*. Firstly, because much partnership research in education involves community organizations such as interagency government organization, clubs and businesses. The researchers, community organizations, and schools work together to explore new ways of serving local communities. This benefits not only that particular local community, but other communities with similar needs. Secondly schools involved in research can take advantage of funding and other opportunities that enhance their ability to serve their students and communities.

This more complex answer to the question 'who gets the benefits of partnership research?' – while similar to the simple answer of 'everyone' – also recognizes that researchers and partners get involved in research for different reasons and therefore have different needs. While this has the potential to make the research richer and more accessible to wide audiences, it also presents spaces for conflict and misunderstanding.

Understanding the challenges of partnership research

So far, we have discussed the benefits and importance of doing partnership research in education. There are, however, challenges that such work presents. This book aims to be realistic and usable, and therefore we will be frank about some of the common obstacles that researchers and partners can face when working together. Although we argue that the benefits of being involved with partners in education research outweigh many of the challenges, it is the case that it will sometimes seem easier for a researcher to have full control of the project and distance from the site where they collect and analyse data. Being aware of potential reasons for conflict or obstacles allows both researchers and partners to put pre-emptive measures in place to minimise damage to the research. While we will identify some of the more common problems associated with partnership research here, Chapters 5, 6 and 7 will explore these in more detail and offer productive solutions for working through these issues.

Trust and respect: While it may sound dramatic, many issues in partnership research stem from a lack of trust or respect. Often the lack of trust or respect is not malicious or personal in nature – it is not that the partners and researchers distrust or disrespect each other per se – but more likely that they do not know enough about the kinds of work each other do and therefore do not place the same value on the same things. For example, some researchers in education are not trained teachers and therefore do not have a realistic sense of the knowledge and practice of the teachers they are working with. This can inadvertently lead to a lack of respect for the teacher's work, which in turn may cause a lack of trust on the part of the teacher. The opposite is also true as work in the academy can seem mysterious, self-indulgent and irrelevant to practicing teachers.

Communication: Unsurprisingly, lapses in communication can often cause friction in research partnerships. Equally disruptive can be miscommunication, particularly if it causes mistakes. Although communication seems as though it should be so easy these days – with email, online networks, electronic signatures, teleconferencing and so on – it is also the case that people working in different types of jobs have different types of access to, and routines for communication. Teachers, for example, do not spend most of their day in front of a computer. The best way to avoid miscommunication or frustrating lapses in communication is to establish a plan or a series of protocols for contact and communication early in the partnership. A 'contact person' who has easy access to the necessary communication tools in each site is often an effective solution.

Apathy and disorganization: This is a difficult issue to overcome and the solutions are often dependent on the reason for apathy or disorganization. Overwork is a common reason for disorganization. Schools are busy places and research participants in schools are almost never allocated any extra time to engage in the research. Researchers can also be over-committed. The nature of research funding often requires researchers to put in many applications knowing that most will not achieve funding. If they do, however, researchers can find themselves unable to devote the necessary time to each project.

Apathy is altogether a more difficult issue as it often stems from a dislike of the research or a lack of interest. Apathy sometimes comes about when the research participants are involved in the study because they have been subtly told they have to be (rather than because they want to be). This is not only an ethical issue, but can also lead to other areas of conflict such as competing agendas or lack of trust. Thankfully, it is not common – more often all research partners are involved in research because they believe it has relevance for them.

Competing agendas: Most people get involved in research because they think the topic is important and want to find out more about it. However, almost no one gets involved in research solely for this reason. Politics of participation and ownership are influential for all members of a research team. For most researchers, researching is part of their job or study and there are expectations about the quantity and quality of the research, by their employers. Partners become involved in research for a variety of reasons. For many schools, it is to improve a particular aspect of their school's performance, or to fulfil funding obligations. Therefore, research participation becomes part of a school plan or performance report. Other partners may be involved to gather evidence about the effectiveness of one of their programs, potentially to apply for further funding, or to attract more interest in their offerings. None of these reasons, in and of themselves, are problematic provided the first reason (belief in the importance of the work) remains paramount. These differing motivations, however, do have the potential to cause conflict. It may mean that the priorities, or the way each participant requires the research to be disseminated, are different. Or it may mean that one participant has a specific requirement (such as the collection of test data or inclusion of a particular programme) that might not align easily with the rest of the research. All participants in the research need to be open about why they are participating and these discussions happen early in the planning phase – different agendas in research are normal; competing agendas can cause problems.

Adverse findings: Depending on why a partner or researcher is involved in the research, adverse findings can appear anywhere on the spectrum of 'extremely interesting' to 'catastrophic'. There are rumours (rarely confirmed) of research that gets 'put in a locked drawer' because it reveals issues that the funding body or partner do not want public. Usually, if this is a possibility then partners will ask researchers to sign a confidentiality clause and so the reaction to adverse findings will not be a surprise. More often, adverse findings place themselves at the 'uncomfortable' or 'undesirable' end of the spectrum for partners. Conflict can arise when partners decide they do not wish to be known as research partners (which can be an ethical issue if they have funded the research) or when partners impose restrictions on what researchers can publish. More surreptitious (and potentially pernicious) alterations like minor word changes to 'soften' language might be made before reports are published. The researchers and the partners, who plan to publish from the research need to have a plan for managing such interventions in their work. If there is a possibility that partners will react unfavourably to findings that do not meet their agenda, then a direct discussion needs to take place. Minutes taken at these meetings can avoid misunderstandings and are good practice.

Relationships are central to partnership research. As we have already argued, this is one of the reasons partnership research in education can be productive and far-reaching. The centrality of the relationships in partnership research, however, is also why conflicts and challenges can arise. It's essential for all members of a research team to realize that research partnerships are not accidental – they are made and managed. Decisions about how these partnerships are made and managed should be direct, clear and made early. Most research that gets done is funded and developed because it is worth doing. In education this means that the research we do can have profound effects on the way schools are organized and the opportunities available to young people, and the way students are taught. Research that is hindered by unnecessary conflict is a wasted opportunity. For this reason, it is imperative that researchers and partners are aware of potential challenges and manage these productively.

Partnership research for powerful change

In this opening chapter we sought to bring together a variety of theoretical, practical, political and personal ideas that inform the 'research space' in schools. Through this, we address what we think are some of the key issues educational researchers working in partnership with schools regularly face. Many of these ideas are recruited once more in other chapters in this volume, often in more depth and detail. We have positioned partnership research as informed by critical education, concerned with praxis, reflection and communities of practice. This theoretical underpinning informs, either explicitly or implicitly, the ideas in this volume. The following chapters draw on these initial discussions to outline and expand issues and ideas related to the roles, responsibilities, methodologies and practical procedures associated with partnership research in education.

Key messages from the chapter

- Education researchers have an ability to make knowledge matter because they work directly with school leaders, teachers and students who are at the forefront of applying policy in diverse communities. This means that for new knowledge and ideas to matter in education, they must have practical and theoretical significance for a range of levels in the system.

- In a very real sense, the new knowledge and understandings created by research in education can change the way young people are taught, the way teachers engage in professional development, the way curriculums are planned and the way schools engage with their local communities.

- Although partnership research in education may emerge from, or orient to, a variety of theoretical and empirical paradigms, it is often informed by notions of praxis – the combination of theory and praxis. Historically, methodologies such as participatory action research have emerged in direct response to the complexities of engaging in partnership research in education.

- Methodological choices need to respond to the particular context and objectives of the research, and 'evidence' in our field should be broadly understood.

- Challenges in partnership research can emerge from a variety of issues, including: lack of trust or respect, miscommunication, apathy and/or disorganization, competing agendas, and dealing with adverse research findings.

CHAPTER TWO

Partnerships: A multi-layered approach

Research is a messy business. For someone who does not know much about research that may seem an odd statement. Despite the planning, preparation and resourcing that characterize a research study, the implementation of research can seem chaotic. Plans vary, data can uncover unexpected outcomes, communication can be difficult, and relationships change. To a new researcher this may seem a little overwhelming. This chapter, while acknowledging the inevitability of a little 'untidiness', attempts to disentangle the 'messiness' of research and map the terrain of partnerships. This chapter also outlines our attitude in doing partnership research; a macro view of the layers of the partnership and the qualities of the researchers within these partnerships.

The qualities of a partnership researcher

There are no definitive lists of what makes a good partnership researcher but there are in our experience certain characteristics that will support the creation and maintenance of high quality partnership research. Here are some of the features that we have noticed in successful partnership researchers.

Passion

It may seem odd to list passion first in our qualities for partnership researchers. To some this may seem the exact opposite of what research should be. Passion, however, is not the enemy of good research. It is one of the key drivers of research that seeks to make meaning in the context in which it takes place. By passion we are not suggesting that the researcher should dispense with reason. On the contrary, reason and a drive for integrity is key to effective research. What we mean by passion here is the energetic pursuit of meaning in the face of obstacles.

Personality experts discuss two types of passion: harmonious and obsessive. While obsessive passion tends to be ego-invested and displays a rigid persistence toward the activity, harmonious passion allows engagement in the activity willingly, and engenders a sense of volition and personal endorsement about pursuing the activity (Vallerand, Fortier and Guay 1997). This is a crucial distinction for those undertaking partnership research. Beyond the glib exhortation to be passionate about our work, this research uncovers one of the crucial factors in the success of passionate individuals. The identification of obsessive passion also provides a salutary warning for researchers who become unhealthily driven by their work. Burnout is an issue in all professions but the demands of partnership research are not suited to all researchers and can lead, if left unchecked, to obsessive behaviours that precipitate burnout and other health issues. As Vallerand and colleagues suggest:

> Passion is a double-edged sword. On the one hand, one type of passion (obsessive) is conducive to burnout, whereas on the other hand, the other type of passion (harmonious) prevents its occurrence ... Because passionate workers deeply care about their work, the challenge for them would appear to remain harmoniously passionate for their work while refraining from becoming obsessively passionate. (Vallerand et al. 2010: p. 312)

Partnership researchers require harmonious passion because it will sustain them through the difficult phases of the research. Partnership researchers require a passion for working together with others in the community but also a specific passion that relates directly to the issues they are researching. According to Vallerand et al. (2010) the key to maintaining and achieving effectiveness and staving off burnout is to ensure that your passion is motivated from your own volition and choices as a researcher. Dewey argues (as we do) that passion and curiosity are a formidable (and rare) combination. He argues:

> In a few people, intellectual curiosity is so insatiable that nothing will discourage it, but in most its edge is easily dulled and blunted. .... Some lose it in indifference or carelessness; others in a frivolous flippancy; many escape these evils only to become encased in a hard dogmatism which is equally fatal to the spirit of wonder. (Dewey 1910: p. 33)

The forging and maintenance of research partnerships requires a sustained energy and a determination to create meaningful understanding and perhaps change for the communities that the research serves. There are easier ways to build a research career than partnership research. So when the challenges inevitably come, the partnership researcher will need a foundation of passion to support her ongoing drive to make a difference.

Curiosity

> The curious mind [is] constantly alert and exploring [and] seeking material for thought, as a vigorous and healthy body is on the *qui vive* for nutriment [sic] . . . Such curiosity is the only sure guarantee of acquisition of primary facts. (Dewey 1910: p. 31)

Research stems from curiosity; we are curious about the world and research it to generate knowledge and understand it better. Educational psychologists have confirmed in psychometric research that curiosity plays a large part in academic performance. In a recent study von Stump et al. (2011) found that curiosity or as they call it 'the hungry mind' made a substantial contribution to performance. The inspiration for many research projects probably emerges when the hungry mind of the researcher coalesces with an understanding of how the research might be delivered and made possible.

In partnership research it is usually necessary to build teams that have a shared curiosity about the issue being explored. As teams research they will find their curiosity is stretched and reshaped by the nature of the partnership and the nature of the research. As this happens it may be worthwhile returning to the initial source of your curiosity about the research. This has two functions; it reminds you of your initial enthusiasm and interest in the research and it helps control the scope of the research by revisiting the initial questions. This is not to say that partnership research cannot grow and change, it can and to a certain extent must. There does come a time, however, when researchers need to 'ring fence' their curiosity to ensure the project does not become unworkable. While curiosity is essential, an ability to know how to channel curiosity will ensure that the research team and the partner do not become overwhelmed by a project whose scope has unsustainably expanded.

Guided subjectivity

For partnership researchers, subjectivity can be both a strength and a limitation of the research method. In much partnership research, researchers, participants and partners are seeking a multidimensional understanding of a problem that is commonly understood through a multiplicity of experiences or realities. The patterns that emerge from this kind of research provide material for contrast, comparison and analysis. Researchers need to acknowledge that their own subjectivities and their own analysis is also unashamedly subjective and is seen through their own political perspective and socio-cultural lenses.

Imagination and creativity

This quality may not be on most lists of qualities for successful researchers but it should be.

Alfred Whitehead (1967: p. 139) argues:

> This atmosphere of excitement, arising from imaginative consideration, transforms knowledge. A fact is no longer a bare fact: it is invested with all its possibilities. It is no longer a burden on the memory: it is energizing as the poet of our dreams, and as the architect of our purposes. Imagination is not to be divorced from the facts: it is a way of illuminating the facts.

A key aspect of an effective partnership researcher is the ability to imagine how a link with the profession can bring about a successful collaboration. The next step is to connect with a like-minded partner who is energized by the vision and can help bring the project to reality.

What this looks like on the ground is hard to define but there are several examples of creativity and imagination being a central feature of the development and delivery of a research project. One example is the Glebe pathways project explored in Case Study 1.

Case Study 1

Case study name: Glebe Pathways Project.

Grant funder: The Australian Research Council, Linkage Grant (2009–12).

Research team: Debra Hayes (The University of Sydney) and Jill Blackmore (Deakin University).

Partners: 'Glebe Pathways Project Forum' compromising:

- Sydney Secondary College – Caterina Di Girolamo, Candace Dower, Jan Flanagan, Jeff Hockey, Janelle Scott, Janine Williams
- Save the Children – Gareth Jenkins
- Glebe Youth Service – Kieran Kevans, Roelof Smilde
- NSW Department of Education and Communities – Eleonora Tojic, Doreen Wilson
- City of Sydney (Sydney City Council) – John Maynard.

Location: Glebe, Sydney NSW, Australia.

Brief project description: The Glebe Pathways Project (GPP) is concerned with the provision of alternative education programmes for young people who are disengaged with school. The suburb of Glebe is an inner-city Sydney

Case Study 1

suburb with a complex socio-cultural and socio-economic structure. The accommodation in the area ranges from housing commission flats to multi-million dollar homes. Many of the wealthier families, however, opt to send their children to private schools while the local public schools have gained a reputation for serving the disadvantaged community in Glebe. The GPP saw collaborations between local schools, universities, education systems, council and the local youth centre to establish a programme to serve young people who were at risk of leaving, or had already left, school. Amongst the participants were students from Glebe's Indigenous community, who have dropped out of education without completing secondary studies. The programme provided these young people with a personalized, problem-based curriculum that aimed both to provide them with 'life skills' and to re-engage them with mainstream schooling. While the central aim of the Glebe Pathways Project was concerned with providing alternative, and personalized curriculum for young people, the project has also been involved in a local campaign to encourage more families in the area to consider the local school as a viable option for their children.

Discussion: The scope of Glebe Pathways Project offers an excellent example from which to discuss the collaborative nature of partnership research. The provision of an alternative educational programme and curriculum required a diversity of expertise in initiation, development and implementation. The partners included a city council, a university, schools, philanthropic organizations and large non-government aid agencies. Professor Debra Hayes who is one of the researchers from The University of Sydney wrote on the project blog about the collaborative nature of the project:

> As the Glebe Pathways Program is a community-based learning program, the development and maintenance of different parts of the program is a collaborative undertaking that is shared among the partners. For example, Sydney Secondary College and the Glebe Youth Service have accepted responsibility for the day-to-day running of the program. The University of Sydney is supporting the professional development of teachers and the implementation of the curriculum. The City of Sydney is coordinating communication among the partners. Community volunteers have taken up a range of responsibilities including guiding governance, mentoring teachers and students, and supporting the breakfast program. (Hayes 2010)

Developing and sustaining the different parts of the project requires innovation and creativity to design new practices and processes tailored to the specific needs of the students within the context of Glebe while making use of the available resources.

Case Study 1

The type of innovation and creativity that is required in a learning environment is largely shaped by the type of curriculum that is being implemented. Personalized learning requires different pedagogical and leadership practices to problem-based learning, or skills-based learning. It is sometimes possible to adopt designs that have been shown to work elsewhere but the unique setting and context of the Glebe project call for more purpose-built designs. Figuring out how to develop and sustain the parts of the project requires a number of problems to be worked on simultaneously. This requires coordination and communication (Hayes 2010).

For us, the salient point of Hayes's description is the way the programmatic and research features of the project are intertwined. In partnership research there is little or no difference between the project and the research in terms of the qualities needed to understand, negotiate and deliver them. They require flexibility, innovation and creativity. There is also at the base of this project a commitment to change the very nature of schooling through partnership action. As Hayes argues:

> Collective educational capacity now relies more heavily upon enterprising coordinated local responses by broad-based collaborations, such as the Glebe Pathways Project. While these types of responses can ameliorate some of the effects of the shrinkage of systematisation, their efforts are not sustainable without ongoing funding, which mitigates the effects of markets and the promotion of the interests of some groups in society over others. Leadership within the radical centre offers a means by which governments, academics and communities can work together to achieve their goals. (Hayes 2012)

Further information: Acknowledging the diversity of audiences for the findings of this project, the team has successfully communicated information and results in a variety of ways. The project has its own website (http://pathingtheway.blogspot.com.au/) with project information, updates from the researchers and links to relevant sites. There is a celebratory video including photos of young people participating in the programme on YouTube (http://www.youtube.com/watch?v=TkidalbxW48&feature=email) as well as a variety of academic publications that draw on the findings from this project (see Hayes 2011 and 2012).

Praxis oriented

Many of the projects we identify in this book have a strong connection between theory and practice. Partnership or practitioner-led research is often thought to be light on theory, but that is a misunderstanding of the power of partnership research to forge strong theoretical understandings that are driven and informed by practice. Theory matters because it provides a way for scholars, practitioners and policymakers working in different systems to speak with a common understanding that is not necessarily context dependent. This allows our research to reach beyond the confines of our classroom, our schools and our nations. Theory can be defined as a coherent description and explanation of observed phenomena that can also produce predictions about the behaviour of individuals or groups (Kettley 2010). Given the usefulness of theory as a way to have rich and deep conversations, you might think it would be a standard fixture in education. The reality according to Kettley, however, is that we are in a state of crisis: 'the crisis of theory building in education studies arises from the failure to encourage original interpretations of data among new researchers. Cleaving to existing concepts and isolated paradigms is not imaginative thinking' (Kettley 2010: p. 9). Theory building in Kettley's terms is a predominant feature of many partnership research projects. Theory should not be accidental or an afterthought but rather a strong and identifiable feature from the inception of a partnership research project. While it may not matter a great deal to some involved in the research, a contribution to theoretical development is a vital part of a researcher's work, whatever field they are in. Returning to our case study, there are explicit and demonstrable links made between theory and practice that emerge from a partnership research project. Here the Glebe project team explains why the interaction between theory and practice makes a difference for all of the stakeholders, not just for the academic researchers involved:

> partnership and associated interaction between practice and research, and between teachers and university academics, provided a site for both the production and application of knowledge. Our argument is that this interaction constitutes a form of professional learning for all participants. This exchange of ideas across institutional boundaries contributed to the processes of pedagogical and curriculum renewal in the schools, as well as to research about changing forms of pedagogy and curriculum in schools. What was critical to the exchange of ideas was the aligning of both horizontal and vertical discourses within school and university systems. (Mitchell, Hayes and Mills 2010: p. 509)

The theory-building in this project informed all aspects of the research and demonstrates praxis in action. The theory developed here has real implications for the practice and professional learning of the researchers and the partners in a symbiotic relationship.

Problem manager

By this term we mean problem solver in the research sense; someone who has the ability to think imaginatively about how and why we create new knowledge in education. We also mean someone who has the ability to sense problems in the research relationship and negotiate a way through them. On large and complex partnership research projects there can be agendas that conflict because the needs of the partner may be different from the needs of the researcher. It often seems like the institutions that are involved in partnership research are like massive cruise liners that occasionally look like they might collide. They are hard to turn and often the passengers (the researchers and the partners in this metaphor) can do nothing to change the course of the ships. For instance, we have both been involved in research that has involved lawyers in the negotiation of intellectual property rights between multiple universities and multiple partners. The simple fact in both cases was that the intellectual property in question was not valuable in a commercial sense. Nevertheless, the lawyers argued endlessly about it. The researchers present were so frustrated by the intransigence and absurdity of the situation they almost left the meeting in disgust. The issue was resolved through the researchers negotiating directly with the partners (without the lawyers) and then informing the lawyers of the outcomes of the negotiations. Essentially, the researchers needed to manage this situation proactively and creatively to forge a solution to enable the research to take place. You will also notice that we have not called this quality 'problem solver'. The term 'manager' has its issues but it does suggest that problems are a persistent and to some extent predictable feature of partnership research and they can be managed.

Persistence

While we were compiling the list of qualities we debated a quality that we variously called persistence, resilience, perseverance and determination. We settled on persistence but these other traits are implicit in our understanding of this quality. In some ways persistence is complementary to passion. While passion provides the initial spark, persistence gets the research designed, partners found, and the project completed. Anyone with even a little experience in partnership research knows that there are many who will say 'no' before you find someone that says 'yes'. So in the initial stages you need to persist through the knockbacks. There are many researchers with stories of 'what might have been' if they hadn't been knocked back by this partner or that funding agency. Part of the research landscape for all researchers, whether they tell you or not, involves harsh criticisms, fair criticism, unfair criticism, near misses, illness and so on. To make a career as a partnership researcher it is necessary to understand that these issues may arise and they require a persistent researcher to ensure that the work meets the needs of all those involved.

The layers of partnership research

We have introduced the concept of layers to attempt to untangle the complexity or messiness of partnership research. While all research is potentially multi-layered any research that engages directly with humans and human interactions provides a special kind of complexity. While, for example, research into pure mathematics has its own complexities, the challenge in partnership research is in understanding all of the audiences or stakeholders of the research and meeting their varied and often specific needs. This section will examine how all of these layers interact in the development, deployment and dissemination of partnership research. (See Figure 2.1.)

Curiosity to inquiry

Let's begin from the bottom of our diagram, with the spark that is often responsible for beginning a research project – curiosity. Anthropologist and

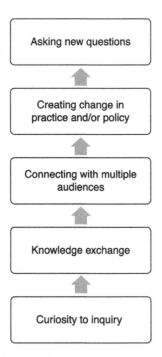

Figure 2.1 *The layers of partnership research*

novelist Zora Neale Hurston argued: 'Research is formalized curiosity. It is poking and prying with a purpose' (Hurston 1996: p. 143). When it comes down to it, most of the partnership research we see emanates from at least a twinge of curiosity, or a series of questions about what is happening in their classroom, or their school or the education system more generally. At various times education research has been prompted by questions that begin with 'I wonder', for example: 'I wonder why so many teachers drop out of teaching?' or 'I wonder if the way young people see their futures is influential on their life outcomes?'. Predictably these questions get more specific and measurable when researchers actually engage with the logistics of designing the research, but they always start from a place of wonder. To illustrate how the process of curiosity to inquiry works it might be worth drawing on our experiences moving from curiosity to a formalized process inquiry. In 2005 Michael was sitting in a theatre surrounded by young people wondering how engaged or disengaged in the show they were. This led to a curiosity about why there had been so little research done in Australia in this area. Many years later the moment of wondering resulted in a large and complex piece of partnership research: TheatreSpace. This research involved eighteen partners, three universities, ten academics and many research associates and assistants. This 'octopus' of a partnership research project with its many tentacles, enormous scale and reach, began because Michael found others in universities and industry who shared his curiosity.

Case Study 2

Case study name: TheatreSpace.

Grant funder: The Australian Research Council, Linkage Grant (2009–12) Total funds AU 3.1 million.

Reseach team: John O'Toole (The University of Melbourne), Kate Donelan (The University of Melbourne), Angela O'Brien (The University of Melbourne), Christine Sinclair (The University of Melbourne), Robyn Ewing (The University of Sydney), Michael Anderson (The University of Sydney), John Hughes (The University of Sydney), Noel Jordan (Freelance, formerly of the Sydney Opera House), Bruce Burton (Griffith University), Penny Bundy (Griffith University), Madonna Stinson (Griffith University), Clare Irvine, Tim Stitz, Ricci–Jane Adams

Partners:

- The Australia Council for the Arts
- Arena Theatre Company (VIC, Australia)
- Bell Shakespeare (NSW, Australia)
- Brisbane Powerhouse (QLD, Australia)
- The Arts Centre (VIC, Australia)

Case Study 2

- Sydney Theatre Company (NSW, Australia)
- Queensland Performing Arts Centre (QLD, Australia)
- Malthouse Theatre (VIC, Australia)
- Queensland Theatre Company (QLD, Australia)
- Melbourne Theatre Company (VIC, Australia)
- Arts Victoria (VIC, Australia)
- Arts NSW (NSW, Australia).

Location: Three large Australian cities – Brisbane, Sydney and Melbourne.

Brief project description: The Theatrespace project is primarily concerned with understanding how young people access, react and respond to live theatre performances. There were two main research strands in the TheatreSpace project: individual case studies that were integrated through national cross-case analysis and a longitudinal component conducted across the three states. Both strands involved qualitative and quantitative data gathering and analysis.

Twenty-one case studies of performance events were undertaken with industry partner companies and venues. A case study research night or matinee performance was chosen in consultation with the partner organization that in many cases selected the performance to be researched, mindful of the particular composition of the audience. At the selected case study performance, as many young people (14–30 years) as possible were surveyed in the foyer before the show. Young people were also invited to participate in an interview directly after the performance, and if not convenient, then over the phone or face-to-face in their schools in the days following the performance. School groups attending the designated case study performance were contacted by the industry partner prior to the performance and once consent was granted the TheatreSpace team liaised with that school via their principal and relevant teacher/s. Young people attending in school groups were generally interviewed twice, directly after the show or in the days following the performance, and where possible, two weeks after the performance. Six month follow-up interviews took place with a small sample of respondents, subject to availability and willingness to participate.

In the Eastern States Longitudinal Study, each state team visited between five and seven schools. The schools were selected based on a number of factors: co-education, single sex, government, independent, catholic, metropolitan, regional, and socio-economic status. Year 10 and 12 English students were given a questionnaire that asked about their live-entertainment choices. Young participants were also invited to participate in longitudinal interviews over the subsequent three years, with consent from their parents/guardians if they were under 18. This research strand was designed to capture responses of young people not necessarily attending theatre.

Case Study 2

In both research strands interviews were conducted with key adult informants – teachers, creatives (including directors, playwrights and actors), and theatre company personnel (including artistic director, and general, education and marketing managers).

Discussion: TheatreSpace is an example of what is possible when multiple partners from geographically dispersed areas collaborate to create a project that responds to a need that has been identified by industry and the partners. TheatreSpace was, and still is as far as we know, the most comprehensive Australian study exploring the arts in the lives of young people. In fact, it is one of the largest studies undertaken in arts education internationally.

You might imagine a project of this scale emanated from a long-term strategy hatched by influential figures, but like many projects it grew from the seed of a few notes on the back of a beer coaster in a theatre green-room meeting between Noel Jordan who was Producer, Young Audiences at the Sydney Opera House (who became a partner investigator on the grant) and Michael Anderson from The University of Sydney. From that initial stage, the development of the TheatreSpace project experienced some serendipity along the way. There was a group of interested academics willing to work with each other; this group were well connected to industry partners who all agreed that a longitudinal study on young people and theatre was timely and required. On the face of it this might not seem so extraordinary, but in the ferociously competitive worlds of both universities and theatre, partnership and collaboration is often the exception rather than the rule. The partners and the universities agreed that we were at a critical moment in time where a substantial piece of research might be possible to support the theatre sector develop tangible outcomes for young people and the theatre industry.

The scale of the project was overwhelming at times and it took some time to move from the curiosity of the initial idea shared in that green room to the actual research project. The building of the team, the support and the resources can have the effect of diminishing the initial motivation to do the research. It took two applications to get the funding from the Australian Research Council. After the first application round, the feedback on the first attempt was applied to the reworking of the application and it was successful in the second round. The grant and the subsequent research was successful partly because the research team and the partners maintained their curiosity and their passion for the project and managed the tedious but essential work of drafting, redrafting and reapplying for the funding that would transform our initial curiosity into viable research.

Further information: The TheatreSpace research was disseminated and communicated in several ways. The project team built in several 'industry

Case Study 2

events' to communicate the findings and their relevance to the theatre sector. Some of these sessions are available on the TheatreSpace website (http://www.theatrespace.org.au). The team is now disseminating the outcomes of the research to the academic community through journal articles (Martin, Anderson and Adams 2012; and several others forthcoming), and through an edited collection describing and analysing the work, *Theatre and Young Audiences: Accessing the Cultural Conversation* (forthcoming, Springer) and several research reports and case studies that are publically available through the TheatreSpace website.

People are curious about all sorts of things- so what separates curiosity from inquiry? Inquiry emerges when researchers put structures around their wondering to seek answers. Essentially all projects begin with an idea. If the idea requires resources beyond what the research has available, then partners and/or collaborators are sought. Together this team grows the idea into a project. Here we see that curiosity becomes inquiry when the components of the research start to fall into place. The construction of inquiry has several features, but here in précis are some of them:

- *Defining the questions and sub-questions:* This is the essential first step in managing the scope and breadth of the partnership research. The questions should be framed with the needs of the partner and the researcher in mind.

- *Choosing research methodologies that suit the questions and sub-questions:* The methodologies chosen should relate directly to the questions being posed in the research.

- *Deciding on the scope of the research project:* the question should determine much of the scope the partner and the research team ought to discuss what resources they can devote to the project and decide how the project will be scoped (for instance how many students surveyed or interviewed, what ages and how often).

- *Building the team for inquiry:* Part of the process of designing and scoping the partnership research project is to create a team that meets the needs of the research question. For instance if your partner requires research into language proficiency in the classroom adding a researcher in linguistics will support the aims of the research.

- *Creating relationships with partners:* The development of strong and enduring relationships with partners will not only create productive associations with the partner on the current project but may set up an enduring relationship to support a long-term research collaboration.

- *Finding funding for the research:* While the partner will usually contribute, it is often necessary to seek external funding from third parties to meet the scope and aims of the research. Many national research councils provide schemes to support partnership research.

- *Understanding and connecting with the audiences for research:* It is critical to understand who will be interested in the research findings and consider how the research design will ultimately connect with its potential audiences.

After inquiry has been formalized, the next layer is the development of processes for co-constructing the knowledge between the partner and the researcher. We are calling this knowledge exchange.

Knowledge exchange

The term 'knowledge transfer' has been used in universities for a decade or more to describe the process where knowledge developed in research institutions can be transferred to industry to assist them. For instance, advances in techniques to treat cancer developed in the research lab can be transferred to medical professionals to support with their work. Of course it is never this simple and knowledge generation in the professions is interactive. A more appropriate term for this process is partnership research knowledge exchange, representing a more democratic and symbiotic relationship. The relationship here is less of the high-status researcher with a white coat observing an objective reality but an imbedded researcher offering knowledge and ideas as well as receiving them. Successful partnership research often relies on an exchange of ideas between the researcher and the partner. Partners have a richer understanding of the realities of their context. In the TheatreSpace project we could not have undertaken the research without the knowledge and skills of the partners. The theatre companies provided us with their own specific knowledge about who comes to the theatre and why. They acted as interpreters; marrying their contextual knowledge with the theoretical underpinnings of the project to gain deeper insights into our research questions. Knowledge exchange should occur frequently throughout a partnership research project to ensure the research is relevant to the sometimes-changing needs of the partner.

In practice this involves mapping the knowledge and skills that the partner brings to the partnership research project. In the TheatreSpace project everyone involved mapped not only their questions for the research but also the resources they thought they could contribute to the research partnership. Knowledge exchange is a constant process in the partnership research relationship and should begin from the planning of the project. Let's explore a hypothetical example to examine the processes at work here. Suppose your research project is a multi-method (including quantitative and qualitative approaches) examination of how effectively science is being taught in schools. The first step for the research team is to discuss the research questions and the space for inquiry. Using our science example:

- Is it a question about primary schools or secondary schools or both?

- What areas of science learning is the research project exploring?

Once the research questions have been explored thoroughly, the scope of the study needs to be explored, for instance:

- How many students in how many sites?

- What methods will be used and in what combinations?

The partner's input in these areas is crucial. Partners have specific knowledge that applies directly to the questions and logistics of the research. In our science example, if the partner is a government organization concerned with disadvantaged schools, the answers to these questions will be different to a science teachers' professional association looking at curriculum development in the area; which in turn would look different if the partners were a business interested in promoting their own educational programmes. In any of these cases the partner should be involved in the early phases of research development to ensure the research meets their needs.

An element of knowledge exchange that is sometimes overlooked is the management of expectations between the research team and the partners. One of the roles of the research team is to control the scope and keep the research project achievable. Sometimes partners have expectations of researchers that are not feasible within the constraints of research funding. Occasionally partners imagine that universities can design, implement and deliver research for almost no cost. Similarly, researchers may imagine getting access to schools and other educational settings is a simple task but our experience suggests that access is often difficult, requiring negotiation and various clearance procedures. This layer of partnership research requires careful planning and negotiation and draws on the pool of knowledge of both the partner and the researchers.

Connecting with multiple audiences

Beyond the partners there are several other audiences for partner research. We discuss in some depth in Chapter 10 various ways of disseminating your research, but before we get to the practicalities of the communication of the research its worth considering the implications for having multiple audiences for your research. Communicating your findings to a wide range of audiences can create a more sustained impact for the research, allowing the work to inform policy and practice across the field. One role of the research team is to consider how best to articulate the research to different audiences in ways that are relevant to them. This need is especially critical in partnership research because the findings are often directly applicable to the profession.

When we are talking about communicating findings for different audiences we are referring primarily to the dissemination of outcomes of the research. There is, however, value in sharing the research goals during the project and to engage or interest the different audiences for whom the research is relevant. Returning to our science education example there are obvious audiences including academic peers and partner organizations. While the partner who invests the time and money in this research obviously deserves 'first look' at the outcomes of the research there is also a responsibility on both the partner and the researcher to feed into the practice of science teaching more generally. The advantage of doing this for the partner is that they can be identified and identify themselves as leaders in this particular area. If the study has international implications they have the added advantage of creating a profile as an international leader for their organization.

Beyond those audiences, however, there are several groups that partnership research may have some influence on. The teaching profession generally has a keen interest in the exploration of key questions that relate to their professional practice. Influencing the practice of teachers is rarely as simple as publishing a journal article and hoping it will generate change. If your research touches on practice it may be useful to design a series of workshops or learning strategies that demonstrate the outcomes of the research in action. This approach fulfils one of the most underrated roles of the partnership researcher – as an interpreter of the research. In this instance the research is being interpreted to support the practice (science teaching) that it has emanated from. There may be some who argue that this 'dumbs down' the research and is reductionist. On the contrary, we feel that interpreting the research to make it relevant to various audiences, in relevant ways, achieves the central aim of partnership research – it makes knowledge matter.

Another influential audience for partnership research in education is school leaders. Rarely is change possible in educational settings such as schools without the support of its leadership. This audience requires communication about the research that meets their needs for curriculum reform and school organization. While the workshops suggested earlier might be of some relevance for this group, it is more likely that communication that is more readily digestible and implementable will meet their needs more effectively. In our science example this could include an executive summary of the research with key findings and a series of practical leadership implications.

As we mentioned in Chapter 1, policy has a complex, sometimes problematic place in educational change (Elmore 1996). A challenge for researchers is to influence policy development through research that emerges from the realities of practice in schools. Sometimes arranging a meeting with senior bureaucrats or politicians is a challenge in itself. More often than not these audiences will be oblivious to the problem, let alone the implications for your research on the solution. One approach is to enlist a 'high profile champion' for your cause. In the science example this could be a leading environmentalist, a celebrity scientist, a prize winning physicist or perhaps a politician. Arranging a meeting to communicate the impact and the 'so what' of the research in a way that is concise and oriented toward specific reform with concrete proposals is key to engaging them in action arising from the research.

A way to reach a variety of audiences is through the media. In our experience journalists sometimes complain that academics use too much jargon, with too much equivocation about their work. This equivocation is sometimes motivated by the complexity of the research and its multiple features. While we are not suggesting that researchers should diminish the scope of their work, it is possible to communicate simply and clearly even the most complex piece of research. Unlike reporting to academic audiences it is not necessary in a media piece to discuss all aspects of a research project (theoretical underpinning, methodology, data collection and so on). We suggest when communicating with the media that researchers relate one or two main narratives rather than attempting to cover the whole project. For instance, using the science research example, talking about the power of using practical excursions in science, such as exploring physics through riding rollercoasters or understanding wave power through swimming at the beach is a clear, meaningful and accessible story to tell a broad range of audiences. Those interested in the complexity and breadth of the story beyond the narrative can access more information through the project's website and other publically available material.

In our experience, researchers in education often express a frustration that their work does not find an appreciative audience and does not make enough of a difference to the educational landscape they research. Perhaps a more thoroughgoing and strategic engagement with the multiple research audiences might resolve some of this frustration.

Creating change in policy and practice

Most researchers do research because they care about it. They hope their research will make a contribution to reshaping their field. In education, as O'Toole and Beckett (2009: p. 8) argue,

Some participation in social reform is part of our raison d'être, either at the level of helping to improve the social understanding, communication skills and interpersonal relations among our students, or making inroads into the greater injustices in society. If you are intending to change society you need to know what you are up against and to monitor and evaluate your success in achieving the changes.

For the most part, our partners have similar motivations in research. Perhaps not always with the same activist stances some researchers carry. There is however, usually a genuine desire on behalf of partners to create research that understands current practice to create better practice for the benefit of those in education. Research does not always succeed in reaching these lofty aims. For there to be any chance of success we need to understand, as O'Toole and Beckett (2009: p. 8), what we are up against. We are up against the policy settings and political agendas, but also the intransigence of a field as large and complex as education.

Therefore, the first part of the process is communicating the outcomes of the research to the multiple layers of the field. To achieve this, a partner's perspective is crucial. While researchers are often adept at identifying themes, trends and approaches, the partners will have the 'on the ground' understanding to manage the change process that emerges from the research. The TheatreSpace project outlined in Case Study 2 discovered that young people often felt that they were segregated from the rest of the audience and made to feel 'other' or 'special' (not in a good way) as an audience. Finding this, the research team explored ways that the ushers might be trained to support young people to feel more comfortable at the performances they attend. This translated into new training for theatre ushers that is now being implemented in the partners' venues. This small example demonstrates practice change arising from evidence generated from research. There are larger reforms flowing through the TheatreSpace research project and many examples of how research more generally precipitates large-scale change in policy; however, there are plenty of cases where this does not occur. So why does some research translate in to reform while other research languishes on the shelf gathering dust? We have no definitive answers to that question but our instincts tell us that research that is effectively integrated with a partner who is motivated to make a difference can effect change. Integral to this change is the deliberate planning with a partner for the change to ensure that the outcomes of the research are relevant and applicable to the field more generally. In our view, if it is worth undertaking the research then it is worth spending the extra effort making it relevant and influential for policy and practice.

Asking new questions

It has become somewhat of a learning and research cliché that 'the more you know, the less you know'. Perhaps a more relevant formulation of cliché that is the more you know the more questions you have. Any inquiry that has sufficient breadth and depth will unearth a host of new questions. This is one of the joys of being a researcher. The glorious uncertainty of what you find leading to more glorious uncertainties that leads to further research. In this sense, research is the ultimate form of lifelong learning, prompting new questions as answers emerge. For the curious, this is the exciting part of the research role. For partners this can be less exhilarating. Partners often carry a desire to have finite findings to support their change process. This can cause a disconnect between partners and researchers that needs to be managed. Many partners, however, understand that implicit within the answers they receive will be new questions, and that education, like any human endeavour, is a dynamic process. Organizations that understand this can create a culture of research that informs practice rather than a series of ad hoc research projects that lack a coherent plan. A partner who is able to ask new questions after research is the kind of partner who may be able to create sustained and sustainable change in an organization.

Features of a multi-layered approach to partnership research

The layers that we have described here are foundational to sustaining and growing in partnership research as a feature of a professional researcher's career. As we move through this book we will fill out more of the details of these approaches but this chapter sought to identify the layers that when taken together, describe a functional and engaged research relationship. In the next chapter, the roles and responsibilities within partnership research are discussed and we continue to consider what we believe to be the crucial qualities of effective research partnerships.

Key messages of the chapter

- There are no definitive lists of what makes a good partnership researcher but from our experience passion, curiosity, guided subjectivity, imagination and creativity, being praxis oriented, the ability to manage problems, and persistence are useful predispositions for engaging in partnership research.

- Communicating your findings to a wide range of audiences can create a more sustained impact for the research, allowing the work to inform policy and practice across the field. A key role of the research team is to consider how best to articulate the research to different audiences in ways that are relevant to them.

- It is possible to untangle partnership research by understanding its layers. These layers include; asking new questions, creating change in practice and/or policy, connecting with multiple audiences, developing knowledge exchange and moving from curiosity to inquiry.

- If it is worth undertaking the research it is worth spending the extra effort making it relevant and influential for policy and practice.

- Effective partnership research will uncover more questions in the planning and execution of the project.

CHAPTER THREE

Roles and responsibilities of partnership research in education

This chapter looks more deeply into the different roles and responsibilities in partnership research. We begin by providing a broad view of the partnership research process and with the potential stakeholders and relationships. We acknowledge that, like most things in education, different local sites and different types of research will have different needs, roles, challenges and outcomes. As part of this macro view, we will introduce key concepts, such as ethics within partnership research and general roles and responsibilities.

Once we have established some of the broader concepts and concerns associated with roles and responsibilities in partnership research, we will explore three areas in more detail. Firstly we outline what we believe to be important practical considerations in partnership research: the culture of the research institution and partners; goal setting, including shared and separate goals; and the development of explicit expectations. Secondly, this chapter will explore the concept of sharing. Sharing is a feature of partnership research and can include the sharing of resources, staff, intellectual property, and knowledge exchange.

Essentially, this chapter is about who does what in partnership research. Specifically it is about how the multi-layered nature of partnership research explored in Chapter 2 requires a thoughtfulness about what roles and responsibilities are important when undertaking partnership research in educational settings.

Roles and responsibilities – the broader view

Before we delve into the ethical and practical considerations of partnership research, we want to outline some of the implicit roles and layers within a research project. As we discussed in Chapter 2, effective research is concerned with a series of professional relationships. Relationships that are between the partner and the researcher, between the research participants and the researcher, between the researchers on the team (collaborators), between the researcher and the audience and between the researcher and his/her peers. We have mapped these relationships in Figure 3.1.

In Chapter 2 we introduced the concept of layers to disentangle the complexity or messiness of partnership research. These relationships connect to make research in education multi-layered for the stakeholders and the audiences it serves. All research is complex and multi-layered; certainly any research that engages directly with humans provides a special kind of complexity. Partnership research in education, however, also requires an understanding the varying audiences and their often-specific needs. The interactions in Figure 3.1 are an attempt to capture the associations between research relationships, research processes and research audiences.

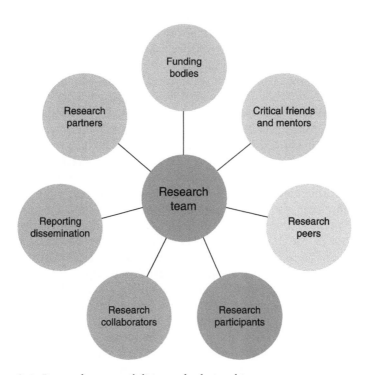

Figure 3.1 *Research responsibilities and relationships*

Researcher, research team, research partner, participant, funding body – these are all roles we have explored far in this book, sometimes interchangeably, to indicate differing roles, responsibility and involvement in the research process. The original title of this section was *who is involved in partnership research?* We felt, however, that the answer to that question was either too simple or too complex to be condensed to a few paragraphs. Obviously, anyone who needs to be involved in partnership research will be; beyond that, anyone who the research team wants to be involved can be (providing the feeling is mutual). So instead of writing a long, and potentially inadequate list, we've decided to focus specifically on roles and responsibilities in partnership research to provide a discussion that is both broad in its ability to be relevant to multiple types of research, and nuanced enough to be practical and useful. The following general overview of some of the roles and responsibilities in partnership research needs to be taken with a proverbial grain of salt, as projects differ across education. The overview should, however, provide some common language and understandings about roles and relationships in partnership research.

The *researchers* in a research project can refer to anyone involved in all phases of the research – conception, planning, implementation, and reporting. This does not mean that all researchers need to be involved in the same way or to the same level; rather, it is concerned with the investment in, and ownership of, the ideas and purpose of the research. These researchers, together with anyone employed specifically to manage or support the research, such as a project manager or research assistants, make up the *research team*. The research team are the people who are central to the research, and for whom the research is central to what they do. *Research partners* generally include organizations that have a clear stake in the research – such as a school participating in the research, a government office who has commissioned or partnered with the researchers to undertake the research, or a private organization who has a key interest in the research. Usually partners are either financially involved, significantly involved as a member of the research team, or both. While these partners can be *funding bodies*, there are also many funding bodies who may call for proposals of research to fund, but will have little, if any, actual involvement in the research process once the funding has been allocated (the Social Science and Humanities Research Council in Canada is an example). Most research in education involves *participants*. Research participants are referred to in this book as those that are involved in the data collection phase of the research, and depending on the methodology this may range from allocating a lot of time and being central to the research design (for methods such as design-based research), to being one of many research respondents (for methods such as large-scale surveys). There is much recent work that focuses on the importance of participant voice in research (e.g. Jackson and Mazzei 2009), particularly student participants (e.g. Bottrell 2011).

There is an emerging research interest in the role of children and students in the research process, with many researchers calling for more attention to 'participant voices' in the design and reporting of research. For the purpose of semantics, in this book 'participants' are distinguishable from members of the research team in their level of involvement. Essentially research participants are asked to contribute to only one or two phases of the research and tend not to have influence over research design.

Researchers have *roles within roles*. Being a researcher is not one thing – it has multiple roles and responsibilities subsumed under the one title. Some of these roles are dictated by the type of and reasons for the research being undertaken. For instance a researcher may assume the role of advocate, provocateur, mediator, translator or consultant. When engaging in fieldwork, researchers may become active participants, reflexive observers, instigators, interviewers, teachers, and so on. These roles should be responsive to the needs of the research and the research context and may shift or become more complex throughout the fieldwork. 'Complicating this ... researchers may occasionally become involved in playing several roles simultaneously with different research audiences' (Adler and Adler 1987: p. 14). With research roles in partnership research being so complicated, these brief and fairly 'efficient' paragraphs on how we are using and defining terms such as researcher, partner and participant are potentially inadequate. We need, however, to be able to use these terms throughout the book with some consistency, while acknowledging that the terms are not static and will shift as we as a research community establish new understandings of the roles and develop nuanced research practices.

The worth of partnership research – ensuring broad benefits

The evidence-based discourse in policy formulation in the field of education has led to a more crowded research agenda. Increasingly, education practitioners are asked to be familiar with research, implement work informed by research and follow research structures to 'prove' the worth of the work they do. While there are many benefits of a more praxis-based approach to schools, this new discourse can also be problematic. Firstly, when research agendas are dictated to local sites it can cause a disconnection between the goals of the researchers and participants, the research, and the work happening in the local sites. This can cause, at best, ill will, at worst, bad research and teaching practices. Secondly, the increased focus on educational research can cause research fatigue in certain sites – particularly those in targeted communities (such as economically disadvantaged communities). There is an ethical issue that must be considered before beginning research. The issues include:

- praxis, and the ability of the research to be meaningful to those involved;

- purpose and goals, and how the research will serve the needs of the research team, the participants, and the local sites of the research; and

- research fatigue, and whether benefits of participating in the research will outweigh the time and energy required.

Before asking researchers to be involved in research, we ask partners and participants – they must establish the worth of the work. As we have said before, schools are busy places. We should only add to the wonderful, dynamic noise and clutter of a classroom when we are deliberately and thoughtfully making knowledge that matters. The remainder of this chapter explores some of the practical ways we can ensure that partnership research benefits everyone involved.

Roles and responsibilities – the details

This section details what we believe to be some of the important practical considerations for a research team when beginning to plan a partnership research project. First and foremost, it's important to *establish shared goals*. Most often, these goals will revolve around the key ideas in the research such as: student achievement, more active school-community relationships, more student involvement in activities, student retention and so on. Conversations with the research team and participants often begin with the establishment of a shared goal – what the research is about and the central research questions. There may also be other shared goals that could be practice-centred, such as establishing a new programme, policy, framework, or approach. Shared goals may also include responses to policy, particularly research involving education reform, or shared funding objectives. In early meetings with all research stakeholders, a vision statement, research purpose, or series of research targets should be discussed and developed. Everyone involved in the planning of the research should be given a copy of these and the opportunity to query or add to them. This document can be useful throughout the research process – it can be used to solve conflict, to make changes to the research plan, and to evaluate the on-going success or otherwise of the research. In our experience, starting with a document for discussion is more beneficial than beginning the conversation with a blank page. Box 3.1 provides an example of this, which could serve as a template for initiating such a discussion.

Guiding questions – initial research meeting

1 Why do you or your company want to do this research?
2 What are you hoping the research will achieve?
3 Will you be using this research for a specific purpose? (Such as applying for on-going funding or to meet policy guidelines.)
4 Is there a particular research question or focus that needs to be included in the project?
5 Is there scope for other questions or foci in addition to this/these?
6 Where is the funding coming from?
7 Are there any implications or requirements from this funding source?
8 What are the parameters for the research (such as particular groups or data to be investigated, enforced timelines, budget)
9 Do you want the research team to design the research with your goals in mind, or do you want substantial input into the design of the project?
10 Who will be in charge of each aspect of the implementation?

Initiating discussions – first research meeting

As well as establishing shared goals, it's also crucial to *outline and understand any separate goals* held by members of the research. To a certain extent, separate goals are inevitable and only an issue if they are in conflict or if members of the research team are unaware or 'locked out' of those goals. As we have said many times, people and organizations get involved in research for different reasons. Most often in partnership research, these interests align but manifest themselves in slightly different ways in the different research sites. For example, research that has student achievement as its central idea may involve:

- teachers for whom the main goal is getting their students to engage more in class, and therefore might focus most on the aspects of the research that the students appear to respond well to;

- school leaders whose goal may be to improve school ranking or test scores, and so might require, or push for, standardized student testing to be part of the research plan;

- academics who are mainly interested in what type of classroom activity strengthens what type of achievement, and so wish to focus on classroom observations and interviews with students and teachers;

- policymakers who are interested in developing and circulating frameworks for improving student achievement, and so require less nuance and decisions that work for broader, rather than local benefit.

So while the central goal may be shared, these different foci mean that different participants may be working on different aspects of the research. While this can cause conflict if not managed properly, it can also strengthen the work by making it multi-layered; speaking to the needs of both local sites and broader communities.

In the past we have used informal contracts to define the research relationship. In this contract we would ask all concerned to spend some time reflecting on the strengths and weaknesses they bring to the project and to think about the ways other project team members could help them to overcome their weaknesses (in ways that were productive rather than judgemental) to keep the project on track. We are not suggesting all research teams write and sign a contract for working together (although we are not convinced it is a bad idea), rather we are suggesting research teams consider their reasons for getting involved in the research, and the main things they want to get out of the research. The different foci can then be managed and negotiated. In the student achievement example provided, for instance, a research method that allows for pre- and post-testing as well as more qualitative data collection could be agreed on. The teacher could have strong input into which students are chosen for the study and what activities are included in the work, provided they connect with the main goals of the research. Timelines and plans that include the writing of the report, the development of a framework for an application, conference presentations, and journal articles could be agreed on, including allocating different writing duties for different members of the team. These negotiations should take place early in the planning process so that everyone involved understands the priorities of the research team and what to expect from the research.

Another practical issue that needs to be explored is *the culture of organizations* involved in the research. It may seem like a fairly elusive and ill-defined element to be placed in the 'important practical considerations' section, but the culture of the organizations in which the researchers and partners' work are significant for how things get done – particularly when it comes to responsibilities within research. There has been much research, in a variety of different professional settings, into the influence of workplace culture and effectiveness, including productivity, inclusivity, retention and safety. In education writing and research, school culture has received a lot of attention recently – particularly as it relates to student achievement, teacher recruitment and retention, and school leadership. Public attention focused on teacher and school quality has resulted in policies calling for increased transparency around the ways in which schools attempt to improve their practices, particularly as it relates to the use of school funding (e.g. COAG

2011). Involvement in research projects, as a participant or a partner, is one way that schools promote themselves as change-oriented.

This raises a fundamental question – how much *should* the culture of the involved organizations matter? To what extent do researchers need to be aware of the culture of the organizations, particularly any potential 'cultural clashes'? And to what extent should it be explicitly discussed in the planning and development stages of a research programme? Although it may seem logical to always have open and frank discussions with research partners and participants regarding the why and how of the research, care needs to be taken when approaching subjects such as school culture. We believe researchers should be:

- Sensitive to the needs of the research partners. Part of this is being sensitive to the fact that the research partners/participants may be involved in the project for different reasons and may be involved despite opposition to this particular project or research more generally in their school/organization.

- Aware that the participants might be involved 'against their will' or for political reasons. If the organization contains elements of bullying from leadership (and this, unfortunately, does happen), or if there is pressure for the researchers or participants to prove something through their involvement in the research, this may hinder the planning, outcomes and sustainability of the work.

- Critical of their own organization's culture. There can be pressure placed on researchers to conduct particular types of research for particular purposes, to bring in research dollars, and to 'publish or perish'. Researchers should be aware that the point of partnership research is that it is conducted in partnership – the school and research partners are not just there to serve the researchers' purposes. Researchers should acknowledge the affects that the culture of education research and academia has on the research process.

When research is hindered by cultures that are dominating, anti-research and/or unstable, members of the research team need to be reflective and ensure that adjustments are made to suit the particular climate in which the research is undertaken. Remember that the goal is to generate knowledge that matters – not just to the partners and not just to the researchers, but also to the multiple layers and stakeholders in partnership research in education.

With these things in mind, how do we *establish explicit roles in partnership research*? We believe it is worth creating specific roles for the team early in the process. That way people know what they are responsible for contributing throughout the process. If you are able to, there are benefits in hiring a research assistant or project manager that works between the sites to assist in developing and documenting these roles. If you are unable to hire someone, then a 'critical friend' from another institution can be useful in these initial organizational discussions. Chapter 7, Delivering Partnership Research will address this question in more detail. We do want to promote the significance of honesty and explicitness. For successful research relationships, all members of the research team need to be honest about their priorities and reflective about any prejudices they may have about the research participants and the work they do.

The politics of sharing

Partnership research is a shared experience. This is one of its many benefits. From conception, partnership research is informed by more than just one understanding of the issues at hand. The research team share their unique perspectives on the issues, their prior knowledge, their particular skills, and their vision for the research from the initial planning phases through to the final report (and beyond). Throughout this process, the research team also needs to find ways to share resources to ensure the research reaches its full potential.

One of the key practical ways that partnership research is shared relates to *workload*. It is not necessary for all members of the research team to have equal workload within the research; rather, an explicit understanding should be reached regarding how much each member is expected to contribute. When having these discussions, it is absolutely imperative that everyone is honest about their ability to dedicate time to the research. In our experience, most workload issues can be easily overcome, as long as everyone is aware of what they are. For example, if a research team knows that the senior members of the team will have minimal time to contribute, they can plan to ensure that they are available at the times in the research process where experience and support are needed – perhaps to have these team members involved in planning and reporting while other members take more of a lead during data collection. Alternatively, if there is concern that everyone is very busy (and let's face it – this is not unusual), then a more experienced project manager might be employed to ensure the research runs smoothly, meetings are productive, and progress is reported regularly. Essentially, being aware of workload issues allows for explicit decisions about who needs to be involved at different times in the research. If all members of the research team are honest about this, and keep the team up to date of any changes, most issues can be resolved.

One way to resolve issues related to workload which has already been alluded to is the sharing of *staff*. By this we mean employing staff to work specifically on the research project. Having a research assistant or project manager whose responsibility is to liaise with all members of the team ensures that all information is going to and from a central point – less information gets lost or confused this way. This is particularly pertinent when there are many people who all require access to research data or documents. Having staff employed by the project also means that there is someone who is constantly 'checking' the research, ensuring that timelines are being met and that participants, partners and researchers are all receiving the support they need to move the research forward. As with any sharing, there can be problems with sharing staff, although we believe the benefits far outweigh these problems. Questions such as who recruits the staff member(s) and where the staff member(s) are located need to be considered with a focus on whose institution is in charge of the project funds, who needs more constant access to the staff member(s), and who has the space and resources available.

The sharing of *space* can be surprisingly political and problematic. Firstly, some organizations do not have abundant space and therefore providing offices, teaching space, or working space can be an issue. In these circumstances it can be easy to create ill will unintentionally if the research is given priority over other space requirements. For example, a school leader who is very involved in the research may inadvertently 'bump' a teacher out of a space to provide those resources for the research, or a teacher who has taught in the demountable classroom all year may question why the research team is given priority access to a classroom. Secondly, the space that the research takes place, particularly the planning, analysing and reporting phases, effects who in the team has continuous and easy access to the research work. Deciding where to place the project manager or research assistant's workspace may seem to be a fairly innocuous decision, but it has implications for how involved various partners feel, and the extent to which partners need to make an effort or be invited to be present at meetings. Pros and cons of different workspaces should be considered and, where possible, shared. One easy way of ensuring this happens is to organize for research meetings to rotate to different venues, or always be held in a more neutral venue. Space can also be considered an important part of how different members of the research team can contribute. Some organizations will offer use of space as an 'in-kind' contribution to the research if they are not able to dedicate as much financial support as other members.

Although not necessarily considered a 'resource', it is imperative that all participants in the research are aware of how the *Intellectual property* of the research will be shared. If the research is funded by an institution (such as a government department of education or university) there will often be specific guidelines or 'rules' about who owns the ideas and results of the research. This can cause conflict when it comes time for institutions to develop contracts about the research – although this conflict may be more between the lawyers of particular institutions rather than the research team, it can cause major delays if it is not resolved quickly. Researchers need to ensure that they are able to publish and discuss the research without breaching intellectual property agreements. This can become critical if the findings of the research are problematic or uncomplimentary of the partner organization. Researchers need to be aware of the extent to which funding bodies can insist on vetting publications or presentations about the research. Researchers working on politically sensitive material may be asked, at the beginning of the research, to sign a 'gag clause' which allows the funding body the right to limit and control public knowledge of the research. While we do not have a personal view on whether researchers should or should not agree to these kinds of conditions, any potential intellectual property issues must be discussed early in the research process. In most cases, intellectual property will be shared, with different partners able to use the research for their own purposes. It may be that this is specifically outlined, for example the funding body may be able to use the findings to develop materials while the researchers may use the research to publish in scholarly journals. In these cases clear expectations around ownership – including authorship and branding – should be negotiated and recorded to avoid confusion.

Key messages of the chapter

- The key relationships in partnership research are between the partner and the researcher, between the research participants and the researcher, researchers on the team (collaborators), between the researcher and the audience and between the researcher and their peers.

- Establishing shared goals will support the integrity and efficiency of the partnership research project. Discussions around the intent of the research and the general and specific research questions will assist in the development of shared goals.

- The culture of the organizations can influence the planning and delivery of partnership research. Different organizations have different expectations in partnership research.

- Effective partnership research is made possible by developing and defining specific roles for the team early in the process. Role descriptions and tagged deliverables for each of these roles will help your team and your partners develop shared expectations.

- Partnership research is a shared experience. From conception, partnership research is informed by more than just one understanding of the issues at hand. Throughout this process, the research team and the partner should work towards ways of working that share information and resources amongst themselves and with the broader education community.

CHAPTER FOUR

Developing a partnership research project in education

This chapter will focus on the practicalities and logistics of partnership research. Partnership research sometimes takes a long time to get from idea to implementation. While in some cases partnership research projects can happen swiftly it is not unusual for partnerships to take two to three years to form and several subsequent years until it produces outcomes such as publications. In essence, partnership research relies on the building and maintenance of complex networks of relationships. Strong networks have the potential to create meaningful and enduring research that is relevant for the partners and the community more generally. Our intention in this chapter is to map out ways of creating productive and sustainable research relationships. To do this, we identify the tacit knowledge of partnership research projects. We identify the processes at work and the skills required to sense the need for partnership research, find the right partners and co-construct a viable and relevant piece of research.

Sensing the potential for partnership research

Sensing the need for research, often referred to as a 'research gap', is expert knowledge that skilled researchers develop over time. Like all expert knowledge, this skill can be deconstructed, understood and therefore learned. One way to explain this skill is to provide an example of the beginning of a small-scale partnership research project. In 2012 a large non-government organization (NGO) in Sydney, Australia had a programme that supported Aboriginal young people to gain confidence and skills in leadership. The programme is described in Case Study 3.

Case Study 3

Case study name: Young Mob.

Grant funder: World Vision Australia.

Research team: Michael Anderson (The University of Sydney), Peter O'Connor (The University of Auckland) and Costa Loucopoulos (The University of Sydney).

Partners: World Vision Australia.

Location: Sydney, Australia.

Brief project description: This research project was generated from a chance conversation between colleagues about a programme that required some evaluative research. Costa Loucopoulos had been working on Young Mob leadership programme which 'enables urban Indigenous young people to develop skills in public speaking and leadership to improve confidence and self-esteem. It also offers opportunities for them to learn more about their Indigenous culture, reinforcing their Aboriginal identity' (World Vision 2013). In this case the research team identified an opportunity to apply an innovative, inclusive and participatory methodology to the research questions. Often the research gap is the 'content' of the research. In this case the gap was methodological and the research team designed a series of methodologies to respond to that gap.

The role of the researchers was to develop a research methodology that suited the unique and specific requirements of the participants and the research partner. World Vision Australia (WVA), which is a large non-government aid agency, approached the researchers to run an assessment and evaluation process. The Young Mob leadership programme had operated for five years and the researchers were asked to investigate how the participants felt about the existing programme and what their aspirations for the programme might be. WVA were also interested in how the Young Mob programme might change to match these young peoples' needs and hopes for their futures. WVA requested a partnership research method that took account of the cultural and pedagogical needs of these young people and provided an opportunity for them to co-design and enact the research. The researchers had all worked in applied theatre approaches in schools and communities for learning and teaching purposes and sensed the potential for the strategies and approaches of this pedagogy to be used for research in many contexts, but especially in our work with Indigenous participants.

The researchers and the partner required a methodology that allowed not just discussion but active co-researcher creation in the research. The Applied

Case Study 3

Theatre As Research approach was an attempt to create understandings that were symbiotic in that it offered an experience that was engaging, culturally grounded and useful for participants. The Applied Theatre as Research process was undertaken on 21 and 22 November 2011. The assessment process began with a meeting at World Vision on 27 June where World Vision Australia (WVA) agreed to use these approaches as part of the assessment process for the Young Mob project. Members of the project team then arranged and convened consultation meetings with Young Mob stakeholders including WVA, teachers and participants to create a research network for the project. The research network approach identifies everyone involved in the research as a co-researcher. This included Indigenous community members who assisted in the assessment processes and gained experience in implementing Applied Theatre as Research approaches.

A series of five meetings of various members of the research network were held to co-create the assessment project. The research/assessment chief investigators (Peter O'Connor and Michael Anderson) negotiated with the key stakeholders the development of a two-day applied theatre programme for Indigenous young people involved in the Young Mob leadership programme to understand what they thought the future could be for the programme. The Applied Theatre as Research approach was explained and members of the research network contributed ideas and approaches to be incorporated into the two-day assessment process. The data generation took the form of role play, music creation, short-film making and poster design where the participants devised art works to respond to the key research question (What works about Young Mob and what is its potential?). The data was analysed to create a research report and a video outlining the process and outcomes.

Discussion: The current Young Mob programme required redesigning to make it relevant for a new generation of young people. The partner wanted to develop an understanding of the experiences of the young participants and how the programme could improve by connecting more effectively with their needs. The partner was concerned that the participants were experiencing 'research fatigue' and therefore sought out a research partner who could engage the participants beyond traditional evaluation methods. The partnership research team worked with the partner to propose a project suited to the needs of both the WVA and the researchers, by delivering capacity building for participants and research outcomes that led to advances in the field of participatory research. The first and crucial ingredient in partnership research is the identification of a shared research need.

Case Study 3

Further reading:

Anderson, M and O'Connor, P. (2013). 'Applied Theatre as Research: Provoking the Possibilities'. *Applied Theatre Research.*

Research relationships

Relationships are central to the success of partnership research. In our experience it is not unheard of but still quite unusual for partnership research to occur without at least some relationship being present. In other words 'cold calling' organizations to offer partnerships seldom works. In the NGO example the contact through the PhD student (Costa) who had an existing relationship was crucial in making the research happen. So, partnership research does not always emanate from your direct relationships but often from wider communities of practice that have intersecting needs and are aware of the potential benefits of partner research.

One of the first steps for researchers is to examine their wider networks to discover potential partnership research opportunities. For university researchers, this wider community can be substantial – all those that have been involved in research and practice in different sectors throughout the researcher's career. For instance, in our careers, Michael worked as a teacher, policymaker and curriculum advisor before his career as a researcher. Kelly has worked in schools in four different countries and as a university researcher at four institutions in Singapore and three different Australian states. Sometimes partners seek researchers. In our experience, this happens more to experienced researchers. Those at the beginning of their research career will often need to make the case for the research and themselves as researchers.

So, relationships open the door for discussions around partnership research and have been the genesis of large-scale partnerships that have been sustained over a number of years. It is also worth considering your present web of relationships including your research students, your colleagues in various sectors (schools, industry, etc.), professional bodies (teacher professional associations, teacher unions, etc.). Just recognising that these networks matter is a beginning of sorts. The next step is to perceive the extent to which the people within your network need and want research. It may seem cynical, but an understanding of the extent to which your contacts are able to make decisions about devoting resources to research will serve you well – research is rarely cost-free. After developing an understanding of your professional network, the next step is to understand their research needs.

Understanding the research need

One of the biggest challenges in partnership research is the first meeting between the researcher and the potential partner. This meeting can feel more like a sales meeting than a collegial research discussion. While you may have a good relationship with a potential partner, sometimes they need to be convinced of the benefits of research for their organization. In the same way as researchers enter discussions with preconceptions about partners; partners may have 'baggage' relating to researchers and research. Partners may think researchers are too remote from practice and would not understand the practicalities that schools, teachers, principals and policymakers face. There is also at times nervousness about how research might challenge practice and create change in an organization. Researchers often wonder whether partners understand the processes of research and especially the frustrating timelines that require patience when answers are usually required 'now or sooner'. In the face of this potential disconnect we have found that stating these preconceptions tactfully and dealing with them reflectively can support the development of a viable project. As well as the challenges, researchers should outline the opportunities that engaging in research offer organizations such as:

- providing evidence for the effectiveness of current practices;
- providing evidence for change in policy and practice;
- developing a culture of evidence and research in organizations;
- leveraging research resources from external agencies to support the partner (from government research funding and universities); and
- providing capacity for those skilled in research to reflect on the processes and approaches of the partner for minimal costs.

This initial meeting between researchers and partners, is not simply for the researcher to promote the benefits of their planned research, but also provides an opportunity to listen carefully to the needs, concerns and aspirations of the partner. Listening in this context refers to both hearing what the partner is saying, and also being aware of what the partner is *not* saying. Predictably researchers sometimes enter these conversations with plans for research that reflect their preoccupations rather than the partners'. We are not arguing here that researchers should not attend to their own research strengths and interests – we as researchers are not empty vessels waiting to be filled by any desires the partners have. Rather, these meetings should provide a meeting place between what the researcher has to offer and what the partner needs for the research project to gain initial traction in their organization.

Researchers should prepare for the initial meeting with the partner by familiarizing themselves with the partner organization and their strategic goals and aims. These are often publicly available; for example, departments of education routinely publish priorities that change on triennial or biennial basis. In addition to responding to the political pressures of the day, these policies constrain spending and provide organizational focus for these large partners. The public priorities often do contain perennials such as literacy and numeracy but other areas are routinely cycled on and off depending on the current political climate. When researchers are seeking partnerships they would do well to ensure their understanding of partner priorities is up to date and consider how such priorities are situated in the planned research.

Methodological imagination

The researcher's ability to imagine how the research project might take place, or as we call it here, the methodological imagination, helps the partner understand what is possible. Once the need for research has been established it is up to the research team to imagine what is possible methodologically. By this we mean imagining how the need can be responded to through research. This aspect of partnership research is crucial to creating a project that aligns with the multiple audiences that researchers need to recruit to the project. It needs to speak to the partner, first and foremost, by articulating what is to be gained through the research and how it will meet their often urgent needs for answers. It also needs to speak to colleagues in the field and contribute something beyond the project to those beyond the research.

Moving beyond the first meeting: Creating the research relationship

Once the researcher and partner have agreed that there is potential for a relationship, the next step is to ensure that both the researcher and partner have a shared understanding of what the research will be. In large-scale research projects researchers should write a short and clear description of the research, explaining the scope and sequence of the project. At times, particularly in large-scale research, partners can have expectations that exceed what is reasonable for a project to deliver. The initial description can assist in ensuring all parties understand the planned parameters and deliverables in the project.

This plain-language description not only allows researchers and partners to progress with a shared understanding, it also an executive summary for decision makers in charge of resourcing in the partnership organization. Providing the partner organization with a concise summary of the significance and implications of the research in a persuasive manner will assist all concerned to make informed decisions about the project. We have included an example of a research project précis in Box 4.1:

Box 4.1 An example of a précis of the research project

Project title: Developing young writers: nurturing creative citizenship and engagement through playwriting programmes for young people

Background: There is now overwhelming evidence that arts learning provides academic and non-academic benefits for students (e.g. Deasy 2002; Fiske 1999; Hetland and Winner 2001; McCarthy et al. 2004). Through the arts young people are given opportunities to explore their social worlds and engage with local and increasingly global communities (Freebody 2009). Recently there has been a renewed focus on the development of young writers to ensure the sustainability of Australian writing into the twenty-first century. As the landmark report into arts and education by the Arts Education Partnership argued, exploring specific expressive activities such as playwriting 'adds to the understanding of the cognitive processes engaged in learning and could yield insights important to the quest for effective educational practices' (McCarthy et al. 2004: p. 23).

Research project: This study will explore the specific benefits of young writer development programmes for students in three contexts (Indigenous, rural/remote and urban). The project will frame the discussion of the benefits of these programmes around the following three factors that affect student learning:

1 The development of *literacy related to playwriting* (skills and knowledge including generic literacy skills, and the ability to communicate ideas).
2 *Engagement* in learning processes (specifically related to writing).
3 The extent to which students develop cultural citizenship (Stevenson 1997) through writing processes. According to Stevenson enhancement of cultural citizenship allows opportunity for young people to engage with a variety of cultural techniques ' in order to produce new narratives of the self' including representations of themselves and an understanding of themselves in relation to Other (Stevenson 2003: p. 346).

Methodology: The literature review and negotiation with the collaborating organization/s will inform the shape of the methodology. Given the research

Box 4.1 An example of a précis of the research project

strengths of the team and the likely shape of the research we expect to employ qualitative methods including:

- Focus groups and interviews
- Conversation analysis
- Ethnographic observations
- Analysis of work products (student writing)

Relevant literature: An extensive literature review is currently being under-taken and will be available soon. However initial influencing articles include:

Jeanneret, N. and Brown, R. (2012). ArtPlay: Behind the Bright Orange Door. Melbourne Graduate School of Education, http://education.unimelb.edu.au/data/assets/pdf_file/0004/720688/behindtheBrightOrangeDoorARC.pdf [accessed 19 July 2013].

Donelan, K. and O'Brien, A. (2006). 'Walking in Both Worlds: Snuff Puppets at Barak Indigenous College'. *Applied Theatre Researcher /IDEA Journal* 7, 1–14.

Griffiths, M. and Woolf, F. (2009). 'The Nottingham Apprenticeship Model: Schools in Partnership with Artists and Creative Practitioners'. *British Educational Research Journal*, 35(4) 557–74.

Orfali, A. (2004). *Artists Working in Partnerships with Schools: Quality Indicators and Advice for Planning, Commissioning and Delivery.* Arts Council England.

Stevenson, N. (1997). 'Globalization, National Cultures and Cultural Citizenship'. *The Sociological Quaterly* 38(1), 41–66.

Stevenson, N. (2003). 'Cultural Citizenship in the "Cultural" Society: A Cosmopolitan Approach'. *In Citizenship Studies* 7(3), 331–48.

This brief document was the product of the first meeting with the partner that began a productive, ongoing research relationship. It attempted to situate the research within the immediate needs of the partner but also located it within a broader context to help the partner understand the potential for this research to have an impact beyond their immediate needs. If a partnership research project is to be funded by external government research agencies it is essential that the project can demonstrate some impact beyond its immediate context (in this case on literacy learning, not just the writing of plays). When you have reached agreement in principle over the scope and general approach of your partnership research it is then time to assemble the team to deliver the vision for the research.

Building the research team

There are some partnership research projects that are undertaken between one researcher and one partner, for example a researcher observing classroom interactions. Even in this instance however, there is a team comprising the researcher and the teacher, not to mention the students who are certainly participants and may be (depending on your epistemology) co-researchers on the project. On the other end of the spectrum, there are teams of hundreds of researchers working on large multinational research projects such as we see in the Organization for Economic Cooperation and Development (OECD) Programme for International Student Assessment research. To discuss how to effectively build a research team, we will examine a research project that required a small team of researchers and partners. Building a team is an integral part of your research design and worth spending time and energy to ensure the right mix of personnel for a project. A good research team allows for a positive and productive working environment, making the research less onerous and more enjoyable and successful for all concerned.

Researchers in education sometimes look with envy at the way some science researchers are able to build and formalize teams around their laboratories. In education research our 'laboratories' are not ours to control, they belong to the participants and are concerned not necessarily with the research, but with meeting the needs of the school, teachers and students. As a result, research in education will always be a partnership and because of the multiple sites of our research will necessarily be collaborative.

Sociologists Hunter and Leahey (2008) identified that since the 1950s there has been a rapid increase in collaborative research. They identified that researchers who could access data readily (close to the same or similar sites) and who had methodologies in common were more likely to be productive researchers. While the study was situated in the field of sociology, it raises salient issues for collaborative researchers in all areas. One such issue is the advantages of working with co-researchers who are situated in education institutions and who share methodological approaches. This, however, presupposes that as researchers we get to choose the research question, context and partner and this is rarely the case. Opportunities also exist when we are working with teams and/or contexts that are diverse and removed from our own experiences and methodological backgrounds. In collaborative psychological research, Zittoun et al. identify some of the issues and opportunities when working with in diverse collaborative research teams:

> Where the parties have very different assumptions, they may need to work harder on making their assumptions and expectations explicit so that each understands why the other contributes as they do. In this case, the collaboration may need additional time and flexibility to develop a shared basis for working together . . . Thus, if one chooses to collaborate across disciplines, reflection upon one's research assumptions is likely to be stimulated. Or if one chooses to collaborate with educationalists or health workers, then one will be forced to question the practical contributions of one's paradigm. (Zittoun et al. 2007: p. 214)

While it is tempting to choose a team that is close in terms of proximity, epistemology and background, there are good reasons for creating a diverse research team. As we mentioned earlier, some of these may emerge from external pressures, from either partner or from the funding agency. Funding agencies often require diversity in research to meet a variety of needs and for the research to have as wide a scope as possible. Prominent funding schemes generally include the following criteria, in which each team member is assessed, together used to determine a strong collaborative research team: skill sets, track record, available resources and the ability to collaborate. These criteria are important in and of themselves, but are assessed in the context of the research project and each member's capacity to contribute to the particular needs of the project. Building a strong research team, in light of these criteria and the benefits of working across research disciplines, requires a deliberate and strategic consideration of what members can offer the project. A well-constructed research team not only increases the likelihood of a well-run, sustainable project, but also improves the chances of grant funding success.

Skill sets

As we discussed earlier in this chapter your preferences are not the only influence over the composition of your research team. Often the needs of the partner and the demands of the research questions will determine the skills required in the research team, which in turn will determine the structure of the team. In a recent partnership research project that we were involved with, the partner was interested in whether in-school arts participation led to better levels of students' motivation, engagement and academic performance. In addition the partner sought to understand what specific teaching strategies led to motivated and engaged students. With the research question and the needs of the partner in mind we recruited quantitative research in the area of motivation and engagement to measure the interaction between these factors and arts learning. These team members worked alongside qualitative researchers and an expert in arts education. These measurement experts had no prior experience of arts education but they did have the crucial precondition for collaborative research – a willingness to engage and discuss different methodological approaches. These discussions converged around how the team might create a coherent partnership project that met the specific needs of the partner through the marriage of divergent methodologies. As we mentioned, sometimes the divergent skills of the team can create projects that are greater than the sum of their parts. In this instance all of the team members learnt about different research strategies and traditions. The added advantage for researchers is that they can publish in areas they have not had access to previously and it establishes collaborative relationships that can endure beyond the life of the current research project into other projects. Building teams with divergent skills can help to develop understanding across epistemologies and between colleagues in ways that building methodologically and epistemologically homogenous teams do not.

To create, diverse and rewarding research teams that incorporate a variety of skills as we have just discussed, it is important to deliberately work across methodological boundaries and break through disciplinary barriers. Klein identifies a continuum of interdisciplinarity 'from simple borrowings and methodological thickening to theoretical enrichment, converging sites, and a general shift ... to new "cross-", "counter-", and "antidisciplinary" positions that front the problem of how meaning is produced, maintained, and deconstructed' (Klein 1996). There are benefits in applying this kind of approach to partnership research as interdisciplinarity reflects the realities of the problems that face our society rather than the rather arbitrary silos that institutions create around disciplines. Interdisciplinary research work can play a critical role in questioning and challenging the bounded nature of some disciplinary knowledge and create new ways of finding out and understanding the world (Castán Broto et al. 2009). Beyond these potential benefits, there is currently a pressure on researchers from funders to create interdisciplinary projects.

As we said earlier, for partnership researchers the needs of the partners often compel consideration of multidisciplinary research. In 2012 we began recruiting a team to research how to design education strategies that aimed to prevent violence against women. The potential partner requested research and programmes that could be used in senior school education to transform attitudes especially relating to adolescent relationships between young men and women. The team that was eventually assembled included researchers from gender studies, applied theatre, education and critical studies. No one member had the expertise to deliver the project on their own. For example, the educators (us) knew about school systems and learning resource development, but were not experts in theories of gender and adolescent relationships. Likewise, the gender studies specialist did not have experience working with schools or with arts-based approaches. This small example reflects the realities of research funding. There is little tolerance amongst funders, and to a certain extent partners, for the disciplinary walls researchers build around themselves. Conversely, funders reward teams who can use the resources and relationships of a university to overcome their boundaries and integrate the different capacities and skills from the disciplines to enrich the research project. From our perspective the application process was efficient and fruitful and the disciplinary differences were more than overcome by the collaborative qualities of the group. There are obvious internal challenges to making interdisciplinary research work. These are, however, often outweighed by the opportunity to build research teams that directly meet the needs of the research partner.

Track record

One of the inescapable realities of grant-getting is the importance of a strong track record. While there are examples of researchers who have been awarded grants with little or no track record this is the exception rather than the rule. This may seem to some a cause for despondency, especially early career researchers. There are, however, ways of developing a team that can help you demonstrate to funders that you have the necessary experience (track record) to deliver the proposed research. One strategy is, once you have a relationship with a potential partner, to form collaboration with a senior researcher. Inviting experienced researchers into the research team can provide the project with specialist expertise and experience in successful grant development. In our experience it is much easier to begin collaborating with researchers that you already know through your teaching, prior research, or contact through professional networks than 'cold-calling' an experienced researcher. Professional events such as conferences are useful ways of expanding your professional network and provide opportunities for you to share research ideas and develop relationships. Like engaging partners, building research teams often emerges from pre-existing relationships. That said, it is not essential that everyone knows each other, but it does make things much easier if there are already functioning relationships at the base of the collaborations.

Although senior researchers often bring grant experience, early and mid-career researchers, who have recently worked in schools or other education settings bring a wealth of institutional knowledge and professional networks to the research. So as much as senior researchers have the experience and track record to shepherd a grant through the application process, members at all stages of their careers contribute to the research in unique ways. In our experience connecting with researchers who are more experienced with a more comprehensive track record allows less experienced researchers to learn on the job in a kind of 'wisdom transfer' that is not available if researchers 'go it alone'. We would, however, add a few caveats to this advice regarding the qualities of the experienced researcher that you are considering teaming up with.

Before approaching an experienced researcher it is worth getting some advice about their ability to collaborate and share equally the tasks and the publications that emerge from research partnerships. Although we have faced it rarely ourselves, there are abundant stories about researchers who 'rent out' their track record to partnership research projects, do nothing to support the planning or implementation of the research and then demand top billing on research publications. A few discrete inquiries with colleagues they have worked with in the past will give you a good sense of whether the researcher you have in mind wants a true collaboration. On this issue, it is also important that you provide the more experienced researcher with genuine opportunities to become involved in the work, by ensuring their skills connect with the context and design of the project, and by giving them a clear indication when and how they can be involved.

Another way to approach track record is to build your own track record by applying for smaller grant applications, evaluations and contract research. Being successful in smaller grants, and the publications such grants generate can put early career researchers 'on the map'. This approach can build a body of evidence that the early career researcher in question is capable of implementing and delivering research and then publishing the outcomes. Smaller grants can be more difficult to find and less lucrative but they are for those reasons also much less popular. There is an implicit trade-off here between the effort you will need to expend on applying and delivering the outcomes of the research (which is high) and an early career researcher's need to get 'runs on the board' in research projects (which is also high).

A third option is to work on research projects without any funding. This is often the case for students doing Research Higher Degrees but is also a possibility for researchers working in academic positions and trying to establish networks, experience and publication opportunities. This approach often relies on goodwill from the researcher and the partner, and some degree of sacrifice to make it all happen but it also provides tangible research with tangible results to give early career researchers the skills and experience necessary to demonstrate their track record in research. It may seem difficult to make something out of nothing, but most researchers, particularly those that have undertaken research degrees, have some if not a great deal of experience in making that happen. A major benefit of such work is that there are no funding constraints and so the researcher (or research team) can develop projects based on their research interests.

Research environment

One of the newer criteria sometimes seen in the assessment of research grants is attention to the research environment. As the term is so new there is still some argument about what it actually means or what the criteria is expecting, but for our purposes it is a term that can articulate how suited your environment is to research. Attention to the research environment allows a team of collaborative researchers to reflect on how well resourced and enabled the research team will be to meet the needs of the partner and the research questions more generally. This relates to physical resourcing, such as vehicles, administrative support, space for research and the like but it also refers to less concrete aspects of the environment such as the ability to connect with co-researchers, mentoring for younger researchers and time to engage in the required analysis and discussion of research findings. The environment is actually a useful analogy because it brings to mind all of the elements that make a place feasible for existence. In research the same issues will arise and need to be accounted for in the planning and the grant applications.

Teams working across multiple sites are common in partnership research and while this can be challenging, it does not necessarily preclude being able to make an argument for creating a productive research environment. Developing a strong collaborative network through technologies such as collaborative online workspaces (such as dropbox), video and teleconferencing have now become inexpensive and pervasive. If these environmental factors are incorporated into the planning and design of partnership research projects, these projects are less likely to face communication breakdown and you are more likely to convince a granting body that you are taking the development and propagation of a research environment seriously. While the research environment is a fairly new descriptor of the places and contexts in which we do research, it has forced many experienced researchers to acknowledge and consider the productivity achievable in their research. While the tangible resourcing issues will always be central to the capacity for research to occur, the intangibles such as the collegial support and the opportunity for professional growth are also essential to making your research attractive to other researchers and those who fund research.

Ability to collaborate

Another intangible factor that influences success in partnership research is the ability to collaborate. We have alluded already to this quality, as one of the most important features of success in partnership research. While it would be convenient to provide some sort of measure of collaboration it is not so simple. As a rule of thumb a researcher who you have worked with in the past with little or no difficulty is likely to lead to harmonious collaborations in the future. In our experience harmonious research relationships are often possible with those from very different theoretical, methodological and epistemological backgrounds. As in life there are colleagues who seem easier to collaborate with than others and once you have found a good colleague, effort should be made to stay in contact and find further avenues for ongoing work. This is not to say that you should only work with the same people you have always worked with – finding new colleagues can be an invigorating and worthwhile experience. We are, rather, encouraging ongoing nurturing of good relationships with an orientation to possible future work. While collaboration is obviously beneficial on any team, it is crucial in partnership research because of the need to interact with partners who often require care and diplomacy. As far as it is possible, select a research team that balances the tangibles (track record, access to resources and publication) with the intangibles (ability to communicate and collaborate). Achieving a balance will lead to a more manageable and enjoyable experience for all concerned.

Building a critical community around the research

Most researchers have heard about the role of critical friend. Costa and Kallick define this role as:

> a trusted person who asks provocative questions, provides data to be examined through another lens, and offers critiques of a person's work as a friend. A critical friend takes the time to fully understand the context of the work presented and the outcomes that the person or group is working toward. The friend is an advocate for the success of that work. (Costa and Kallick 1993: p. 50)

We extend this concept a little further by suggesting that most partnership researchers require a critical community for their research. In a way, the critical community is a scaled up version of the critical friend. A critical community is in essence a group of critical friends who can interact with different aspects of the research depending on their expertise and experience. The critical community shares the qualities of the critical friendship but can be called upon to work collaboratively to help to shape and progress the research. The critical community may provide a range of different skills to the partnership research, often to make it robust and relevant to the partner the researcher is working with. The composition, membership and approach of this group will be entirely driven by the needs of the project. For example, if you are doing a piece of partnership research that explores how a large national testing scheme has changed outcomes for students, the critical community may be involved in measurement studies, schools, policy development and so on. In the development of the concept for the research it is worth discussing the ideas with researchers experienced in this kind of approach. These individuals for one reason or another may not be interested or available for the research team but there are many researchers who are happy to play a mentoring and advisor role throughout the development and delivery of a project. On the partner side it might be worth finding someone who works in similar fields in your own country or internationally to provide advice about the needs that have emerged in their contexts and their research questions. This advice can be vital when assembling the initial pitch for the partner for the research project. While many researchers have a strong sense of the needs of partners, this process validates their hunches and increases the likelihood of the project being sustainable in research terms and getting traction with partners. There are several other critical community roles that will support the specifics of the project but they will become apparent when the research begins to form as the researchers and the partners negotiate its scope and parameters.

The critical community can also play an important role acting as an official or unofficial advisory group to the partnership research project.

In all of the large-scale research projects we propose we incorporate an international advisory committee that is another term for the critical community. The international advisory committee (we often use the term international steering committee but the functions and general roles are the same) can provide advice on the design and implementation of the project but can also help to connect your work to broader conversations beyond those taking place in your immediate context. We have included an example in Box 4.2 of the way this kind of group is described in a grant application as it explains the role and the function of the group (personal and institutional pseudonyms are used):

Box 4.2 Descripion of International Steering Committee

An International Steering Committee (ISC) will be convened and will be responsible for advising the project regarding the requirements of the partner organization. The ISC will advise the project about international development in simulation-based games and applied drama. The ISC will consist of the Chief Investigators, the research associate from the partner organization, A/Prof Richard Gutterson (University of Midwest, USA), Professor Steven Sutran (Co-Director, Games and Gaming Research). Associate Professor Gutterson and Dr Elaine Pea will serve as advisers on this project. Specifically, they will: 1) travel to the research site for a three-day meeting with chief investigators and offer advice on the design of the research project and the process of school implementation; 2) participate in a symposium with chief investigators at the internationally renowned Games, Learning, and Society conference in New Orleans in 2017; 3) provide consultation support to the project. This collaboration will promote linkages between the innovations in this project in this country with research into games and learning internationally, assist in connecting the programme to the latest advances in the field as well as supporting the dissemination of the findings from this project to global audiences.

A group such as this signals to grant bodies that the research is internationally relevant and has the capacity to communicate its outcomes beyond the local community. This approach connects the research to a broader range of expertise and understanding and will provide the project with experts and advocates who can support it as it grows.

Conclusions

The partnership researcher's journey is long but it does not need to be lonely. The opportunities available through networks and collaboration make this type of research one of the more communal areas for engaging beyond your own research. We mentioned at the start of this chapter that some researchers in education might pine for the control that the lab offers but it is also true to say that many lab-based scientists look enviously at the work partnership researchers do for its ability to make a difference and for the potential it holds to make change to people's lived experience. And that in essence is the great challenge and the great opportunity of partnership research – the necessity to collaborate, negotiate and create research with others. In the next chapter we discuss how to initiate and lead different kinds of partnership research and manage effective and sustainable research partnerships.

Key messages from the chapter

- Partnership research relies on the development and maintenance of complex networks of relationships. Strong networks have the potential to create meaningful and enduring research that is relevant for the partners and the community more generally.

- Sensing the need for research (the 'research gap') is expert knowledge that skilled researchers develop over time. Like all expert knowledge, this skill can be deconstructed, understood and therefore learned.

- One of the first steps for researchers is to examine their wider networks to map the potential for partnership research opportunities. For university researchers, this wider community can be substantial – all those that have been involved in research and practice in different sectors throughout the researcher's career.

- The methodological imagination is the researcher's ability to imagine how the partnership project might take place. By this we mean imagining how the need can be responded to through research. This aspect of partnership research allows the partner to understand what is possible through the research, which is often different to their expectations (for better and worse depending on the expectations of the partner).

- Once the researcher and partner have agreed that there is potential for a relationship, the next step is to ensure that both the researcher and partner have a shared understanding of what the research will be. In other words what is the scope and the scale of the research.

- A well constructed research team not only increases the likelihood of a well-run, sustainable project, but also improves the chances of grant funding success.

- Partnership researchers can benefit from a critical community for their research. In a way, the critical community is a scaled up version of the critical friend. A critical community is in essence a group of critical friends who can interact with different aspects of the research depending on their expertise and experience to provide research support throughout the design, delivery and dissemination of the project.

CHAPTER FIVE

Initiating and leading partnership research

The nature of a partnership research project changes depending on context. A central aspect of this is how, why and by whom the research is initiated. This chapter is concerned with exploring the ways in which leadership, ownership and initiation of research affects the structure purpose and implementation of projects. To begin, this chapter explores broader issues of ownership in partnership research, considering the position and roles of funders, researchers and participants in terms of ownership and control. The chapter then explores partnership research from two perspectives – initiated and led by a partner organization, and initiated and led by researchers. We appreciate that this dichotomy is somewhat arbitrary as most research will not fall one side than the other, but will fall somewhere in the middle. We split them here, however, to illuminate some of the key ways research differs depending on the nature of its conception, funding, purpose and management. Within the exploration of these two perspectives, common approaches, common challenges, and ways in which the research can make an impact will be discussed. We will also present case studies of two projects – one researcher-led and one partner-led – to explore the practical implications of the key discussion points.

Who owns the research – whose research is it?

For some research, it may be more appropriate to consider who owns what aspects of the research, or maybe to look deeper into the idea of 'ownership'. Although this is a complex issue with many facets, this chapter will focus on three central roles – funders, researchers and participants.

If research is commissioned by an organization, paid for by that organization, and designed to serve that organization, then it is not unreasonable to think of that research as owned at least in part by that organization. This view, however, does not consider the role of the commissioned researchers in conceiving, designing, implementing and reporting on the research; the intellectual property, the decision making beyond the original brief, and the documents produced by those researchers. Likewise, there are questions around whether research can actually be 'owned' or whether all knowledge produced by so many (the research team, participants, partners and so on) belongs more in the public domain. This reaches into more contentious questions such as whether an organization has the right to keep secret a piece of research that they bought and paid for, or whether the academic community has a right to publish research findings that may put a funding organization in a difficult position. Recently, the ownership of research has been a critical issue with a backlash by researchers against large publishing companies. The Cost of Knowledge movement (Neylon 2012) has recently gained widespread support amongst academics who have stopped submitting their articles for publication with the large publishing house, Elsevier. Those behind the campaign claim that research outcomes are becoming cost prohibitive, excluding many from the outcomes of research. In response to this campaign, several government research funding agencies have implemented open access policies to support the publication of work that is after all (at least in the case of government agencies) research that is funded by the public purse. In Australia, The Australian Research Council's policy states:

> The Australian Government makes a major investment in research to support its essential role in improving the wellbeing of our society. To maximise the benefits from research, publications resulting from research activities must be disseminated as broadly as possible to allow access by other researchers and the wider community. (Australian Government 2013: p. 1)

We have a great deal of sympathy for this approach. In our view, if public funding has made the research possible there should be access, at a reasonable cost, to the outcomes of that research. Publishing houses that use academic intellectual property (in articles, books, etc.), and then intellectual labour (in editing and refereeing) and then charge prohibitively high prices for access seems, on the face of it, quite unreasonable. Without wishing to go too much further into this debate these recent developments around access to research signify the strength of feeling on these issues and suggests this could be an issue of conflict in the future.

The position of research participants in the 'ownership' camp is one that is, in our opinion, often overlooked. As we will explore more deeply in Chapter 8, 'Methods for partnership research', education researchers are looking to a variety of strategies and methodologies to understand our field in more depth. Many of these, unlike more traditional large-scale quantitative studies, require significant input, time and effort on the part of research participants.

One of our initial motivations for examining partnerships in research is because, for many education researchers, 'partners', as opposed to 'funding bodies' or 'subjects', is a more productive way of thinking about the relationship between those involved in the research at a variety of levels. Teachers, for example, working on a research project may spend countless hours planning and implementing interventions, documenting student work, keeping journals, liaising with parents, developing resources and much more. In these situations, care and attention needs to be given to questions of 'ownership', 'whose research is it?' and 'who gains?' Too often in education research, the hard work of the participants can be ignored by funding bodies and researchers – with little credit given or appreciation shown to those who are at the centre of the research endeavour.

Having said this, all members of the research need to acknowledge that the 'core business' of the research lies in the generation of new knowledge; the collection, analysis and reporting of data that are productive to the central research questions. To generate new knowledge, in ways that make a difference to the field of education, difficult intellectual work needs to happen. This adds a complexity in answering the 'ownership' question posed above. It is true that research needs funders to resource it, and participants to give their time, ideas, and effort. It is also true, however, that those in the research team that conceive of, analyse and make connections between the raw data, research questions and broader research purpose are undertaking the core business of research – the generation and dissemination of new knowledge.

The relationship between knowledge and money in modern universities is not necessarily an easy one. Researchers are expected to apply for competitive grants and build relationships with organizations that will commission research to fund work and 'bring money in' to the institution. As a result researchers often need to find ways to research the areas they are interested in within the confines of what research they are able to get funding for. This can lead to a compromise in the type of work researchers do and to an increase in researchers interested in more 'popular' areas that are, in turn, more likely to be funded. Whether this is a 'problem' is not something that we wish to make a judgement on, researchers and funders all have differing opinions on the success of this system. It does, however, put pressure on the relationship that researchers have with the research. This is particularly the case when the research in question is paid for by an organization. There are questions around whether paying for research means that the knowledge generated by the research is owned by the organization rather than the researchers or other stakeholders. There are many situations where researchers are asked to sign away their ownership of the knowledge and therefore cannot publish or present on the work without the permission of the organization. These cases are extreme and not necessarily common. It is more common, however, for a funder to require publications be submitted to them for approval before being published. In this case, the funding organization may change wording or delete sections they feel do not reflect them in a positive way. Conditions such as these unsettle many researchers, but are a regular part of partnership research. If your research project is funded through a large granting organization there are protocols and processes available to your partnership research project to deal with these matters.

These issues of ownership and control once again demonstrate the need for all members of the research team to be explicit about their goals in doing the research. When we say 'goals' we mean the research goals (what you want to find out in the project) and the more peripheral, yet powerful, political- or career-driven goals (what do you want the research to achieve for you?). If possible, then, members of the research team need to be relaxed and accepting that different members of the team may have different goals, and try to find ways to make the research 'work' for everyone. This is providing, of course, that the goals do not contradict each other or, critically, that the peripheral goals do not hinder the ability for the research goals to be met. We realize that the importance of shared and separate goals has already been outlined in Chapter 3, but it bears repeating here. Like many other things in partnership research in education, ownership is multi-layered. A researcher who plans to present their work at a conference can be prevented by a funding body if the initial contracts removed the researcher's rights to any intellectual property. Similarly, all publications may require specific authorship (such as a department of education) rather than allowing the researchers authorship. These kinds of issues can conflict with the initial motivations researchers have in a research project. Clear guidelines relating to intellectual property, rights to publish, product or organization branding on public documents and decisions about dissemination (including the right to prohibit or limit publication of the research) should be established early in the process and need to align with the specific shared and separate goals of the research team. Once all these rights and needs are established, research design decisions can be made that suit the requirements of the researchers involved.

Researcher-led research

Firstly, *what is researcher-led research?* Well, as you can most probably imagine, there are numerous different ways this sort of research could look. Essentially, researcher-led research is a research project that is instigated by the researcher (perhaps an academic or research student), where the partner(s) are approached to participate in a project that is potentially already designed. Certainly, in most researcher-led projects the overall purpose and research questions are usually already established before the partners become involved. If the project is part of a larger research agenda, or led by a research student then the research design may already be set, or will certainly be moulded by what is appropriate and achievable in the circumstances. If the researchers are in the process of applying for a grant then the partners may be approached to become involved earlier and have more influence over the design. Using very broad brushstrokes, one of the differences between researcher-led research, compared to partner-led research, is that it usually begins with the research question, rather than an external purpose. Put another way, researcher-led research is often inquiry for the sake of finding out something new, separate from the needs of a particular organization. Researcher-led research is often, though not always, concerned with the testing or development of theory.

The second question to explore in this section is *why do researcher-led research?* Our answer for this is relatively simple – because it's an enormous, and unfortunately rare, privilege. Too rarely in our professional lives do we get the opportunity to follow our own research agendas and explore answers to the specific questions in our field that we find intriguing. More often, we research because someone asks us to, or we apply for grants with proscribed research agendas. Our research, although often relevant and meaningful, is usually a compromise between what we want to do, and what someone will fund us to do (or what our research partners want us to do – which often amounts to the same thing). There is nothing wrong with this – research work is often most meaningful and useful to the field when the purpose and questions have come from practitioners and policymakers. However the opportunity to work on self-initiated research – whether it is a PhD, a post-doctoral programme, or a large funded grant (ESRC, ARC, etc.) allows us as a field of researchers, to explore the areas of education praxis that may be otherwise overlooked because they are too quiet, unpopular, or obscure. It is the opportunity to find new knowledge in the unexplored corners of our field; to experiment with new ways of connecting disciplines within education; and to follow our passion without too much compromise that makes this kind of research so attractive.

For many researchers, the PhD will be one of the only times in their research career when there is the opportunity to deeply explore an aspect of education simply because it is of significance or interest to the researcher. Those fortunate enough to develop their own post-doctoral programme or be successful in large external grant-funding schemes not only get more opportunity to do this kind of work, but, with the additional funding, often have the chance to extend their work to explore research questions more deeply or on a larger scale. Unfortunately, funding for research in education is becoming increasingly politicized in many countries with a focus on narrower aims, objectives and topics. For example, recent Discovery funding for early career researchers in Australia supported only two education projects (out of two hundred) and both were concerned with NAPLAN testing (a government initiative of external literacy and numeracy testing).

A consequence of grants such as these becoming more competitive and more narrowly politicized is that researchers compromise the 'discovery' nature of their work to align with political agendas and preferred methodologies. These broader questions regarding the nature of research funding are potentially a discussion for another book, but are mentioned here because they have consequences for the ways that education, and education research is shaped. Chapter 7, 'Delivering partnership research', explores in more practical detail issues to do with funding researcher-led research.

When it comes to researcher-led research, there are not necessarily a set of *common approaches*. Rather, researcher-led projects tend to take on the form that suits the interests and expertise of the researchers. These projects can range from large-scale survey or intervention studies, to very focused ethnographic studies involving one or two students or teachers. Despite the lack of common approaches, there are a few *common challenges* that researcher-led projects are more likely to face than projects that are instigated by partners or funders. One of these relates to the involvement and investment of partners and participants. Researcher-led projects often require participants to be involved without having input into the design of the research. Indeed, participants and partners are often sought *after* the research has obtained funding and therefore key decisions about purpose, structure and dissemination have already been made. This can mean participants feel they are working for the researchers rather than with the researchers (or for the broader purpose of the research). As we have said more than once already in this book – schools are busy places and education practitioners are often time-poor. For partnership research to be successful, all members of the research team and participants in the research need to feel like the research is worth the time and effort they are investing in it. Whatever the overall purpose of the research project, researchers should consider the particular benefits or outcomes for participants and partners. Researchers need to be realistic about the amount of time and effort required by the participants. Ill-will can be generated when a participant feels like they were not given correct information and are now 'locked in' to a bigger task than they originally believed. Obviously, direct communication about the research purpose, outcomes and expectations is the easiest way to ensure all participants in the research understand and are invested in the work. This communication should be both formal, such as information statements about the research, and informal, such as ongoing information conversations about what is happening in the research, how the research is going, where the research is up to, and any changes to the research plan.

One way to ensure that all partners feel invested in the research is to seek their involvement in the early, planning stages of the project. There are many benefits to this. Firstly, it ensures that the research is relevant to the people it intends to serve. Secondly, it consolidates the partners' participation and gives them the opportunity to have input into the planning of the research to ensure it meets their needs. Thirdly (and by no means lastly), having partners involved in the research from an early stage, prior to *seeking funding*, demonstrates to potential funders that the research has value both theoretically and practically and has the support of the professional community. One potential problem with seeking partner support and input early in the process is that quite often research is not awarded the full funding it is seeking. Partners can become jaded or despondent if they have given large amounts of time and effort developing work that is not successfully funded. Our suggestion, if you are planning on bringing partners into the process early (and many grants will require a demonstration of partner commitment prior to funding), is to ensure that realistic information is given to partners about the chances of the research successfully getting funding. In our experience, it is often worth developing a 'back-up plan' with partners; ways that the research, or a part of the research, can be undertaken even if the funding is not successful, perhaps through alternative funding sources or as a smaller pilot project.

Another challenge associated with researcher-led research stems from the initial theme of this book – how to make the new knowledge matter. Keeping in mind that researcher-initiated and led research does not necessarily come from the direct needs of the partners, the research team should consider how they will *make an impact with the research*. Research that is initiated by the professional community tends to have a ready audience for the research outcomes. By instigating and participating in the project, the research has made an impact on the practice of at least those involved, most likely also those that work in the same school/area/subject. This practical demonstration of the relevance of the work gives leverage in the professional community, allowing the new knowledge and understandings to circulate at conferences, through resource development or professional learning. Research that stems from a more theoretical hypothesis, or emanates from a particular passion or methodological interest of the researchers may require a different approach in dissemination to ensure that it has an enduring effect on the professional community. To be clear, we are in no way suggesting that research necessarily needs to have practical application to 'matter'. There has been a great deal of research that has fed our field philosophically, theoretically, methodologically; made us better and more informed educators. Rather, here we are acknowledging that for research to make us more effective and more informed as a field, it must be accessible and available to the field, and in our field, that often means it needs to be relevant to education practitioners. A plan for dissemination that includes a wide variety of audiences is one way of attempting to make the findings relevant and important to the multiple layers of the education system. We also suggest that the partners and participants in the research are heavily involved in multiple forms of dissemination. As part of the research plan, different partners could take responsibility for interpreting the findings for different audiences – for example, with teachers working in schools, policymakers publishing resources, and academics presenting and publishing in academic journals (we discuss research communication and dissemination in depth in Chapter 10).

Case Study 4

Case study name: Drama and Oral Language (the DOL project).

Grant funder: Centre for Research in Pedagogy and Practice, National Institute of Education (NIE), Singapore with funding provided by the Ministry of Education, Singapore.

Research team: Madonna Stinson (Principal Researcher, Visual and Performing Arts, NIE), Kelly Freebody (Research Associate, NIE).

Partners: The project was conducted through the Centre for Research in Pedagogy and Practice in partnership with the Visual and Performing Arts academic group at NIE and four local high schools.

Location: Four Singaporean high schools.

Brief project description: This project was concerned with the effect that participation in process drama workshops (O'Neill 1995) had on the development of second language acquisition. The intervention took place in four schools in Singapore, working with 'Normal Technical' stream students, which is the lowest stream, in Secondary 3 (students were approximately 16 years of age). Each class had approximately forty students. The intervention groups participated in ten hours of process drama work with a trained facilitator during their English classes, while the control groups in each school attended their regular English classes. Data was collected via pre-tests and post-tests for randomly selected students; facilitators' journals; and interviews with the with facilitators, the students' regular English teachers, and randomly selected students. The intervention included not only the implementation of the lessons but also the planning of the drama work and the training of facilitators.

Discussion: This project was a small-scale pilot study which, owing to its strong findings, was successful and was 'scaled up' into a larger study titled *Speaking Out: An Exploration of Process Drama and Its Contribution to Oracy* which sought to determine how transferable the approach was to the broader school context, and investigate the implications of the approach for teacher preparation. The initial impetus for the study stemmed from the principal investigator's curiosity and expertise.[1] The project gained traction

---

[1] The term 'principal investigator' usually refers to the instigator and leader of the research. While there can be several chief investigators, there is usually only one principal investigator.

Case Study 4

not only because it was a well planned project that aligned with the investigator's skills, but also because it was timely. In 2000 the government had launched the 'Speak Good English' movement, and in 2003, just a few months before this project started, the Singaporean prime minister had reinforced the importance of English to Singapore's future economic growth (Stinson and Freebody 2009). This public concern was recruited by the study to ensure that it was relevant to both the schools involved and the education community more broadly. The principal investigator applied for seed funding from the Centre for Research in Pedagogy and Practice through a competitive application process. As a pilot project, this was successful. Its success can be measured in a variety of ways but specifically, this project:

- Was effectively implemented and produced powerful results.
- Communicated the results to a variety of audiences for a variety of purposes.
- Achieved further, more significant funding, to expand the exploration of the issue.
- Reported on emerging findings from the qualitative data that were in addition to the main findings and research questions. These 'additional' findings were recruited as further discussion in the reporting of the study and were incorporated into the expanded research project.

Further information: Like all partnership projects, different dissemination strategies reached different audiences. The research report for this pilot study (Stinson and Freebody 2004) was central in the acquisition of further funding. The report primarily served the purpose of communicating the results to the funders (the research centre and Ministry of Education) and the partnership schools. The results of this study were disseminated to the academic community through conference presentations (Stinson and Freebody 2006) and other publications (e.g. Stinston and Freebody 2009). This being a pilot study which was extended with a further, larger study, the results of the DOL project are also communicated in publications and presentations focused on the later study (see Stinson 2009 and Stinson 2012).

Partner-led research

When we refer to partner-led research, we are discussing research that is initiated and, significantly, moderated, by the partners. The term 'partner-led' is potentially misleading as often the day to day organization and decision-making is undertaken by the academic researchers, however the distinction between this and researcher-led research lies in the research purpose. Partner-led research is developed by the partner, usually to serve a purpose specific to their needs. Academic researchers are then brought in as consultants with expertise in research, the research area or the research methodology to undertake the research. These projects can be funded by the research partners, by external funding, or a combination of both.

There are several answers to the question *why do partner-led research?* First and foremost, partner-led research often originates from grass-roots issues or needs in the specific research site. As a result, the research can be immediate and relevant to the professional community, providing excellent opportunities for researchers, partners, participants and teachers to engage in praxis. It may also be the case that the issues explored in partner-instigated research are not always those that get the attention of the wider research community. Partner-led research offers researchers the chance to be at the 'cutting edge' of issues that are current and pressing in an ever-evolving education system. Beyond this compelling reason, partner-led research gives researchers an opportunity to engage in new methodologies, new fields and learn new things. Not only are research skills honed, parallels between the partner-led research and the researchers own expertise and passions often help to create new understandings of the issues and allow researchers to engage with the professional community in new ways.

While partner-led research may engage with a variety of approaches and methodologies, there are a few *common approaches* that require the researchers to act more as consultants or critical friends. Methodological examples of this include action research and design-based research, both of which will be explored in detail in Chapter 8. This section, however, will focus on evaluation research as one of the key ways researchers get involved in partner-led research, particularly if the partner is a private organization working in conjunction with the education system, or a school endeavouring to justify or fund its programmes.

In essence, an *evaluation* is a piece of research initiated by the partner that seeks findings that are driven by the partner's needs. In this scenario the researcher is a 'gun for hire' and although a particular researcher may be chosen on the basis of their understanding of the area, they need to be cognizant of the requirements and parameters of the partner and not their own preferences. As the experienced Australian researcher Lyn Yates puts it, those who commission evaluations (or as she calls it contract research) 'are not interested in some abstract ideal of good research, they want research that specifically meets their needs' (Yates 2004: p. 134). While this may sound a little cynical it actually helps researchers to know that the partner may be driven by motivations other than (but not excluding) good research practice, and that partners often initiate research for advocacy or with other political agendas in mind. There is nothing implicitly wrong with research being used for policy and advocacy work. It is in a sense what most researchers would want for their work, and as we discussed earlier, having research affect policy is, in our opinion, an all too rare occurrence. Researchers undertaking evaluations, however, should be careful to remain independent in the process to safeguard their integrity. We are not suggesting here that you should not discuss the research with the partner. That is a little absurd and runs contrary to the kinds of principles we have been arguing for in this book. Rather, there should be an explicit understanding in your discussions with the partner about the purpose of the research/evaluation findings, and your entitlements as a researcher.

With regard to *seeking funding*, evaluations are often initiated through contact from the partners asking if a researcher might be interested in evaluating a programme, or a notice in a newspaper or through the web calling for interested researchers to bid for the evaluation work. If you are aware of a programme you believe may benefit from evaluation then it is not uncommon to 'pitch' your services, although you should be clear about how much the research will cost, and we suggest that you present the partner with various options for funding, including collaborative grants and philanthropic opportunities.

There are many types of and approaches to evaluation, but perhaps the best advice is to make clear to the partner the kind of evaluation you can manage based on your methodological experience. If the partner requires qualitative research and your experience as a researcher is solely quantitative you should make that clear and either find a qualitative researcher to collaborate with or turn down the work. Having established that you fit the requirements of the evaluation you should spend some time understanding the motivations of the partner and negotiating your *process for the evaluation*. Any initial discussion about an evaluation should include:

- The purpose of the research – why is the research being commissioned?

- The audience of the research – who will read or have access to the findings?

- The scope of the research – time and resource allowances, number of participants and so on.

- The required dissemination of the findings – do the partners want a formal report? Will there be multiple audiences for dissemination requiring different formats? Do the partners want video and other materials with the report?

- What are the arrangements for payment – including in-kind aspects such as use of equipment or space.

- What are the compliance expectations on the researcher (ethics clearances, occupational health and safety issues, insurances, etc.)?

- Who will be the person that undertakes various roles within the research – is there a research student or research assistant involved who will undertake the majority of the data collection and collation?

Table 5.1 codifies some of the issues that may arise from the beginning to the end of an evaluation relationship. We have adapted them in this table from Yarbrough and colleagues (2011). In our opinion, these standards are a good guide for researchers who are new to the field to build a framework that accounts for the utility (pragmatics), feasibility, propriety and accuracy issues of the evaluation relationship.

These standards, although specific to evaluation research, have relevance for other types of partnership research. In fact, many of the indicators associated with each standard reflect good research practice more generally. Issues of reliability, fairness, effective reporting and appropriate use of information are central administrative tenets of research. When undertaking evaluation research, part of the agreement is to produce the research results that are 'useful' to the funding organization; therefore, these indicators become absolutely paramount. The effects of not attending appropriately to one of these indicators could be devastating for the research, the programme being researched, and potentially, the research participants.

Partner-led research, as we've already argued, is not only evaluation. It can include research initiated by education departments to explore a particular issue (such as quality teaching), or that undertaken with the aim of producing resources for use in policy or professional development. This research is often more varied in its approach. There are, however, some common benefits and challenges in partner-led research. As outlined earlier in the chapter, much of the *common challenges* associated with partner-led research revolve around issues of control, ownership and communication. The rights and responsibilities of the entire research team (researchers and partners) need to be clear before research commences. While we do not wish to make value judgements on different arrangements, researchers who decide to forfeit the right to ownership or control over the research findings should be aware that they may never get the opportunity to publish or use the results of their research. In these situations the researcher becomes more of an 'employee', undertaking the research for external reasons such as payment or experience.

Beyond the larger issue of control and ownership, more common challenges include the breakdown of roles within the research team. As the instigator of the research, the partners will often want more involvement in the research design, or may have very specific research participants in mind. Therefore, the team needs to have a clear understanding about who will be undertaking different tasks in the planning and implementation of the research and whose approval is required after each step is completed.

Table 5.1 Adapted précis of the programme evaluation standards (Yarbrough et al. 2011)

Evaluation standard	Definition	Indicators
Utility	The utility standards are intended to increase the extent to which program stakeholders find evaluation processes and products valuable in meeting their needs	**Evaluator Credibility** **Attention to Stakeholders** **Negotiated Purposes** **Explicit Values** **Relevant** **Meaningful Processes and Products** **Timely and Appropriate Communicating and Concern for Consequences and Influence**
Feasibility	The feasibility standards are intended to increase evaluation effectiveness and efficiency.	**Project Management** **Practical Procedures** **Contextual Viability** **Resource Use**
Propriety	The propriety standards support what is proper, fair, legal, right and just in evaluations.	**Responsive and Inclusive Orientation** **Formal Agreements** **Human Rights and Respect** **Clarity and Fairness** **Transparency and Disclosure** **Conflicts of Interests** **Fiscal Responsibility**
Accuracy	The accuracy standards are intended to increase the dependability and truthfulness of evaluation representations, propositions, and findings, especially those that support interpretations and judgments about quality.	**Valid Information** **Reliable Information** **Explicit Program and Context Descriptions** **Information Management** **Sound Designs and Analyses** **Explicit Evaluation Reasoning** **Communication and Reporting**
Evaluation Accountability	The evaluation accountability standards encourage adequate documentation of evaluations and a metaevaluative perspective focused on improvement and accountability for evaluation processes and products.	**Evaluation Documentation** **Internal Metaevaluation** **External Metaevaluation**

Some questions to have answered at the beginning of the research relationship:

- How involved in the research planning do the partners want to be?
  - Do they want the researchers to plan and implement the entire study without their involvement?
  - Do they want to be involved in initial planning (research questions and basic structure)?
  - Do they want to be involved in all planning meetings?
- Once the research is planned, who has the final 'sign-off' before the research can begin?
- Who should be copied into email communication and document sharing?
- If the partners are in charge of the programme being evaluated, will they instigate contact with the research participants? Will they choose the participants?
- Who will be in charge of obtaining ethical clearance for the research?
- Who will be named as investigators in the research for any legal documents? Often one person from the partner organization will be a named investigator (they can be referred to as partner investigators or principal investigators). Sometimes, however, the organization would rather not be a named investigator.
- Who will manage the research? Who will be the key liaison between the researchers, partners and research participants?
- Do the researchers have the right to present the work at conferences and publish in journals? If so, does the organization wish to be named as a research partner? Be aware that there are ethical issues associated with not releasing information about research funding – particularly in evaluation research situations.

This is not an extensive list of questions, but will provide prospective researchers with an idea of the type of information that can help a research project run smoothly. For researchers, partner-led research can be an strategic way to develop a rapport with the professional community; engage in targeted, relevant research; and develop publications and presentations around important work. For partners, partner-led research gives credibility to the work they are doing, allows them insight into aspects of their work they may not have investigated fully, and publicize their work in different fields. With so many benefits to the research team, it is crucial that the research meets the standards outlined by Yarbrough and colleagues (2011) in Table 5.1, to ensure that the research project is a productive and supportive experience for those involved.

Conclusions

In many ways, it's easier to *make an impact with partner-led research* than with some other types of research. As discussed, research initiated by a partner has the benefit of being connected to a perceived need that is usually the catalyst for the research. This leads to research with a strong purpose and, usually, direct relevance to the field. It is also often the case that partners will initiate ways in which the research can be shared with the professional field. Examples of this include using the research to develop resources for use in schools or classrooms, professional development incorporating the research findings, development of policy influenced by the research, and the inclusion of the research in events such as teacher conferences. Praxis can be developed when we allow theory and research to influence practice, and practice to influence theory and research. All good research work, whether it is an evaluation, a large-scale quantitative study, or an in-depth analysis, should be founded in theory and should build on what we already know. As a result, all good research work should be shared with other researchers to build a bigger and deeper foundation for our work.

Case Study 5

Case study name: Teachers Research Communities.

Grant funder: Department of Education and Communities (DEC), NSW State Government, Australia.

Research team: Peter Freebody, Kelly Freebody and Beverly Maney (The University of Sydney).

Partners: Priority Schools Programmes, NSW DEC.

Location: New South Wales, twelve 'priority' schools receiving funding for serving low socio-economic communities.

Brief project description: This project was based on the need for a more focused and systematic approach toward greater understanding of community–school relationships and the effects on student engagement, student learning and teacher retention. The theoretical framework of this project draws from the work of Gonzales, Moll and Amanti (2005), particularly their theory of 'funds of knowledge', which essentially relocates the role of teachers as cultural workers in an effort to integrate community knowledge into the policy and practices of everyday schooling. The project involved twelve schools in NSW Australia, all of which were targeted with extra funding for socio-economic disadvantage. The research was in two phases. Phase one of the project involved classroom observations and with interviews with all participating members of the school community including: teachers/executives, students and parents/community members. The data

Case Study 5

gathered was used in to assist in the development of a 'Community Inquiry Framework' (CIF) which aimed to give teachers and school leaders practical approaches, informed by theory and research, to researching their community and developing successful school–community relationships. Phase two of the project involved a series of design-based researched projects incorporating the CIF into teacher and school practice to trial and refine processes and content.

Discussion: This project was, to a large extent, instigated and designed by the partner organization. The partners identified an issue facing schools – new teachers posted to schools in disadvantaged areas were not connecting with the community their school serves. They believed that this was potentially one of the reasons teacher attrition was an issue in these schools. The partner sought researchers to investigate the issue and produce a research-informed framework for community inquiry which could be used for professional development and induction programmes for new teachers in schools. Therefore, the research was initiated by the partners and the research team were approached to do the research. The development of the project was collaborative, with the researchers designing the project around the relatively strict parameters set by the partners, and on the condition that the research culminated in a practical framework for teachers to work with. There are several practical implications of this kind of partner-initiated research. The benefits of such work is that the researchers are, for all intents and purposes, assured that the study is relevant and important to the partners and participants. This takes much of the 'guess work' out of the development of the project. Usually in these projects, as in this case, there is much scope for the researcher to implement a study that meets the needs of the partner while at the same time aligns with the researchers' interests and skills. Often specific researchers are approached because they have a research interest or history working in the chosen field (in this case schooling for low socio-economic communities).

Further information: Like many partnership research projects, there are multiple ways that the outcomes of this research have been communicated to meet the needs of differing audiences. The research report (Freebody K., Freebody, P. and Maney 2011b), literature review (Freebody, P. and Freebody, K. 2010), case studies (Freebody, P. and Freebody, K. 2012a) and Community Inquiry Framework (the final document for teachers) (Freebody, P. and Freebody, K. 2012b) are all available on the DEC Priority Schools Programmes website (http://www.lowsesschools.nsw.edu.au/lowsesresources/Home.aspx). The research has also been drawn on for publications and conference presentations for the academic community (e.g., Freebody, P., Freebody, K. and Maney 2011a)

Key messages from the chapter

- The ownership of research can be contentious. Think about ownership of aspects of the research including who owns the right to publish? Who owns the intellectual property that emerges?

- Participants are often the forgotten people in discussions around research ownership. Partnership research projects can employ strategies to engage participants in the 'fruits' of the research.

- Above and beyond ownership, all parties in partnership research should be committed to the 'core business' of the research – the generation of new knowledge; the collection, analysis and reporting of data in ways that make a contribution to policy and practice.

- Researcher-led research is instigated by the researcher (perhaps an academic or research student), where the partner(s) are approached to participate in a project that is potentially already designed. Partner-led research is initiated and significantly, moderated, by the partners. Evaluations are a common form of partner-led research.

- Evaluation is a piece of research initiated by the partner that seeks findings that are driven by the partner's needs. Essentially, the researcher is hired for their skills and experience for this kind of partnership research.

- Your methodological experience and your understanding of the area for evaluation are key considerations when choosing evaluation projects to engage with.

CHAPTER SIX

Resourcing partnership research

For many partnership researchers it is not the ideas and the imagination for research that is in short supply, it is the resources to make the idea into a research reality. In this chapter we examine some strategies for resourcing a partnership research project. We prefer the term 'resourcing' rather than 'funding' as it acknowledges there are opportunities to do research generated from a researcher and/or partner's own resources that are not always financial. A PhD partnership research project is an example of this. While often resourcing one's own project may not be ideal, it can give the researcher a start and some experience in partnership research that will provide capacities and skills for larger scale research later on in the partnership researcher's career. This chapter will also discuss different kinds of funded research and processes involved in applying for different funding schemes that are available.

Self-resourced research

In the humanities and social sciences it is commonplace for researchers to undertake self-resourced research at the beginning and sometimes toward the middle of their career. While in the sciences research students are often 'attached' to a lab or a project that is already underway, researchers in education often find that they generate their own research project that is funded from within their own resources. We will discuss the specific features and approaches of PhD partnership research in Chapter 9, 'Developing doctoral research partnerships', but here we discuss some of the ways researchers can do research within their own resources more generally. Table 6.1 presents an example of how the budget of a self-resourced partnership research project works in practice. This example is taken from a PhD partnership research project that interviewed four teachers in four separate schools about the effect of curriculum change on their practice. This budget reflects a PhD candidate's budget for the year where data

Table 6.1 An example of a per annum budget for self-resourced research

Item	Cost	Funding source
University student administration fee	$297	Researcher's expense
Photocopying	$500	University allowance
Recording equipment	$400	Sourced from partner
Transport/fuel	$900	Researcher's expense
Laptop computer for data entry	$2000	Provided by researcher's workplace
Qualitative data analysis software (NVIVO or similar)	$1500	Provided under university licence
Referencing software (endnote or similar)	$1200	Provided under university licence
Editing, proofreading	$1500	Researcher's expense
Conferences attendance (Local and International)	$3,000	University Postgraduate Support Scheme
Printing and binding	$650	Researcher's expense
Total	**$11,947**	

collection and thesis submission is anticipated. These figures are approximate but they provide a sense of the proportion of funding allocated to different cost items.

While this is only one example, the table indicates what is possible if the research is designed to take account of low resourcing levels. In this instance the 'researcher's expense' only accounts for approximately 35 per cent of the expenses with the remainder being sourced from the university and the partner, either through in-kind contributions or financial support schemes. A feature of the research in this example is that the project is closely tied to the professional role of the researcher. This allows this researcher to use work trips as data collection opportunities (with the approval of her employer), further reducing the costs of the project on her.

This approach does take some planning but there is commonly a willingness amongst partners and employers to support the research in low-cost ways to ensure that the research and the outcomes of that research are available to the partner. This approach also maximizes the funding available from the university and uses the resources available strategically. Not all universities will offer the same support in the same places so it is worth thoroughly investigating what resources are available before designing the research.

Although the limitations of self-resourced research can often create frustration, sometimes, especially for the early career researcher, they can be the only choice for those without a research track record. We have also used this approach with very small research projects which we think are vital but we know will not attract funding because they do not fit the current internal or external funding parameters of the research granting authorities. Dispensing with external funding can also avoid many of the pressures placed on research projects to produce findings that serve purposes other than those that meet the needs of the researcher and partner. Whatever the case, there are times when this approach to research fits the needs of the researcher and the partner well and can create meaningful and satisfying research experience for all concerned. For larger and more complex pieces of research most researchers are forced to walk the often rocky and sometimes difficult funded-research path.

Funded research

Perhaps the best place to start with funded research is to ask yourself whether you actually need external funding for your partnership research project. As we have indicated in the discussion on self-resourced research there are some projects that may not be possible without funding and therefore it is necessary to expend the time, expense and effort involved in seeking external funding. Grant applications routinely take weeks of development that could be better used actually doing research if external funding is not required.

There are, however, some very good reasons for seeking funding. In the first instance there are partnership projects that cannot be managed solely with the capacities that you and your partners have available. One of the other motivations for researchers to seek external funding is concerned with career building and prestige. While internal grants and self-resourced research are a good place for beginner researchers, there is an expectation amongst employers and colleagues that mid-career researchers will begin to accrue external research grants to support their work. Some institutions put dollar values on the quantum of research funds that is expected of researchers. In our view this is a fairly mindless aspect of the 'career progression game'. Grant sizes do not usually reflect the value of the research, nor their local or global impact. More likely, grant size reflects the priorities of the funding bodies and the cost of the research – this is not the same as the value of the research. For instance scientific research is routinely more expensive than other forms of research. That does not guarantee that the work is more relevant, more applicable or more useful than research in the humanities and social sciences but that is the metric that universities and others that routinely rank research employ to 'value' research. This leads to a kind of research 'arms race' where researchers make ambit claims for research funds only to see everyone cut back. The end result is some research budgets bloating and others getting cut, or not funded to suit the needs of some researcher's careers.

If you do need to apply for funded research there are a few avenues, some well known and others less so, for you to pursue. We have discussed in earlier chapters the different forms of funded partnership research but here we would like to focus in on the specific funding implications for each form using examples to illustrate how to approach the applications.

Developing the application

While we have discussed the potential of self-resourced projects, we realize even though it is possible to do research on goodwill, this does not mean it is resource free. The time and effort taken to develop the project, liaise with the partner, develop the ethics application, collect the data and report on the research all entails a huge amount of resource on the researchers and the partner's behalf. While this might be possible when you are in the early stages of a research career it becomes less feasible as competing demands arise in a mid-career researcher's life. Therefore, researchers who wish to undertake bigger or more complex studies will need to consider the grant application process to fund larger scale research. The first step in acquiring such funding is to map the available funding sources.

Government research granting agencies

Perhaps the most obvious place to start the funding search is the standing research councils that are a feature of most Western research systems. The Economic and Social Research Council in the United Kingdom describes itself in this way:

> We are the UK's largest organisation for funding research on economic and social issues. We support independent, high quality research which has an impact on business, the public sector and the third sector. Our total budget for 2011/12 is £203 million. At any one time we support over 4,000 researchers and postgraduate students in academic institutions and independent research institutes.
>
> We are a non-departmental public body established by Royal Charter in 1965 and receive most of our funding through the Department for Business, Innovation and Skills. Our research is vigorous and authoritative, as we support independent, high-quality, relevant social science.
>
> We offer:
>
> Quality: All ESRC research awards are made in open competition, subject to transparent peer assessment at the outset and evaluation upon

completion. Rigorous standards are applied to all the training we support with other Councils, and frequently takes a long-term view. Our datasets, longitudinal and panel studies are internationally-acclaimed resources.

Impact: Our research makes a difference: it shapes public policies and makes businesses, voluntary bodies and other organisations more effective as well as shaping wider society. Our knowledge exchange schemes are carefully devised to maximise the economic and social impacts of the research that we fund.

Independence: Although publicly funded, our Royal Charter emphasises the importance of independence and impartial research. We have no 'in-house' researchers, but distribute funds to academics in universities and other institutes throughout the UK. (ESRC 2012)

There are a few aspects of this self-description that are worth noting. Firstly there is a large quantum available that is spread amongst a large number of people. At first glance the numbers seem quite impressive but the funding averaged out the amount per researcher that they claim is only £50,750 which, for many research projects, is modest to say the least. The other feature worth noting is that they are interested in high *quality* research that has *impact*. Leaving the discussion of quality to one side for the moment, their identification of impact is germane to partnership researchers. The identification of impact signals their interest in research that suits partnership researchers as we are also interested in understanding impact in educational settings. They go on later to say that their schemes make a difference which, as we have mentioned is the primary motivation for most partnership researchers in education. There are other similar bodies in Australia (Australian Research Council), Canada (National Research Council) and in New Zealand (The Royal Society and The Marsden Fund). This government research is often considered to be prestigious because it is relatively difficult to obtain (the success rate for Australian Research Council Discovery grants, for example, is approximately one in every ten applications). The benefits of such research is that, beyond the initial grant-getting process, the organization is not intrusive and, beyond annual budgetary reports, does not intervene in research planning or implementation.

Philanthropic funds

There are several philanthropic organizations who specifically focus their research on education research. For instance the Ford foundation have a global funding category titled 'Educational Opportunity and Scholarship' that describe their mission this way:

We focus on strengthening educational systems to ensure all young people receive an education that enables them to engage in meaningful work and contribute as citizens in diverse societies.

We work with organizations that produce compelling new thinking and evidence; promote effective and scalable practices; and communicate, advocate, and build the capacity for reform.

Worldwide, we fund initiatives designed to transform the quality of secondary schools and help students from poor or marginalized communities gain access to quality higher education.

In the United States, our secondary education work focuses on expanded and redesigned learning opportunities, high-quality teaching, adequate and fairly distributed resources, and strong accountability.

Our higher education efforts support greater access and affordability, and innovations that increase the likelihood that students will earn degrees.

We also support scholarship and cultivating the next generation of public intellectuals to inform and inspire social justice progress.

In 2012 the Ford Foundation granted $79,352,668 on 240 grants in the Educational Opportunity and Scholarship category alone.

Again the partnership researcher will see much to encourage them to submit an application. There are strong partnership agendas running through the Ford Foundation's self description that refer directly to engaging with and improving practice. These agendas are not uncommon in many philanthropic funding bodies. The question for the partnership researcher is the fit between themselves and the priorities that the foundation has identified. Sometimes fitting a funding organizations agenda is possible by amplifying and reshaping your original idea to fit the needs of the funder. Successful partnership researchers become adept at finding connections between their research interests and ideas and the external priorities of funding organizations. In education, these are often closely matched as many funding bodies are concerned with social well-being and community development – both areas in which education is vital.

Government organizations

There are many government organizations that request research as part of their core business. These departments are often interested in developing research partnerships that extend beyond evaluation of programmes, or require research that can both evaluate programmes and engage in more complex theory-building work. For instance recently, a large government department concerned with creating job opportunities for Indigenous Australians built into a tender a large piece of research that accompanied the employment creation programme. These kinds of research partnerships have some distinct advantages and have some difficulties. Government departments are usually very focused on delivering outcomes for clients. This makes them ideal for partnership researchers in education. They routinely have a clear sense of the outcomes that need to be achieved and they are often working with disadvantaged or marginalized groups. Some may argue that these kinds of research participants are those that benefit most from research. Departments of education, public health organizations, and youth-based government organizations are obvious partners for educational researchers to consider. The challenges can arise when the politics of an organization conflict with the needs of the research and the researchers. If you are considering working with a government organization, you should be aware that even at lower levels of bureaucracy they are often driven by the political whims of the politicians in charge. If you understand this as a researcher, it will make it easier for you to navigate some of the priorities that arise, sometimes without warning, in these agencies.

If you are considering working with the government agency on your partnership research project, ensure that you understand the priorities of that agency and that you have some contacts to help you navigate the organization you are targeting. In our experience, it is very difficult to navigate an agency where you have little knowledge or prior contact. For many researchers in education, their prior professional life has been spent in an education setting as classroom teachers, school leaders or in more bureaucratic policy development roles. This experience is valuable when considering potential partners for your research. It is worth having confidential conversations with contacts that you may have from your previous engagement with government agencies to understand the current priorities and the likely future priorities of that agency. If you have not worked in government previously, that is not necessarily an impediment to working with these agencies. It may be a case of finding somebody to partner and collaborate with that has these contacts, so that you can navigate effectively as a team through these organizations. Whatever the case, if you are looking to work with government agencies it is best to go in with an understanding that bureaucracies have agendas. Some of these agendas will be documented in official documents while others will be hidden from sight.

Developing partnerships with private and non-government organizations

In education research, public sector partnerships are in our experience most common. Partnership researchers do, however, create research projects with non-government organizations. This can range from large NGOs like aid agencies or faith-based welfare organizations to for-profit organizations that require research partnerships to understand more deeply issues relevant to the organization. For instance, large telecommunications companies often require research that supports the understanding of how new technologies might be deployed to create new markets in education. It is important at this point to make the distinction between groups like NGOs and not-for-profits, and organizations that require a return on investment and are motivated primarily by the need to raise revenue.

In our experience NGOs (and other not-for-profits) are usually aligned closely with the motivations for transformation that inspire and motivate partnership researchers. This means in most cases the initial conversations with these organizations require the proposed research to align with the organization's values. Recently, we met with a non-government organization to discuss the opportunities for them to change and enhance their practices. These conversations were around maximizing the impact in the community, not developing or delivering large returns for shareholders. The stakeholders in this conversation were those involved in the research.

Large for-profit organizations are obviously motivated by making a return for their owners. We are not suggesting, however, that this precludes them from being motivated by social change. The development of 'triple bottom-line reporting' (Elkington 1997) has meant that many large corporations are acutely aware of their social responsibilities and are often interested in working with researchers to understand the impact of their work and to mitigate any harm. Sometimes these companies also enlist the support of large NGOs to develop and implement social support services for the companies they work with. Mining companies routinely develop social support policies and implement them in the communities they work with. Whatever the case, understanding the motivations of each partner and their values will help researchers develop projects that meet the needs of the partners and the community they serve. It would be foolish and counter-productive to exclude the possibility of working with for-profit organizations as many of them provide strong partnership opportunities that can lead to productive research projects.

The resources for the partnership

There are many ways to develop a partnership. The following approach reflects the ways that we have worked when resourcing our own partnership research projects. We are not advocating this approach as the only way, we are instead suggesting this is a way that has been useful for us when we developed our own projects. As we have already discussed, the first thing we do when developing a resource plan for partnership research projects is to construct a one-page outline or précis of the project so that we can speak to potential partners about our ideas and attract their attention to the project. The one-page project description should let the potential partner for the research know the what, why, how and where of the project. It is similar in some ways to an abstract or an executive summary that engages the reader. The one-page summary helps the partner establish that the research is relevant to them and fits within their policy parameters. The one-page document is not intended to outline detailed budgetary descriptions of the project, it is, however, intended to position the partner within the research and give them a sense of the budgetary scope of the project. For an example of this précis see Chapter 4. In our view, resourcing matters are best left to the second or third meeting with a partner. If the partner accepts the general scope outlined in the one-page document then a more detailed budget can be prepared for the partner to consider. Partners can be excited about the possibility of research and see the need for it, but when issues of resources are raised they sometimes seem reluctant or unable to make any financial commitment. Although we think it is important to wait until there is consensus and momentum around the research idea before discussing the particulars of resourcing, it is usually worth making it clear from the first meeting that research is a resource intensive and costly exercise that will have resourcing implications for partners. There is no context in which research is cost free, and time taken by you as a researcher to develop a research project that will not achieve funding is time that could be spent doing other things. We often include the following paragraph in our one-page document:

> This research will require financial commitment by the partner organization that may be in cash and in kind or both. The scope and composition of the financial contribution made by your organization can be negotiated as we develop the research project.

This short statement makes it clear to the partner organization that research has a cost and the partner will be expected to bear some of that cost to support the outcomes of the research. While many partners understand this very clearly there are some partners who expect research to be handled entirely from the resources of the researcher and their organization. This is akin to a potential homeowner wanting an architect to design and build a house for nothing. Any research that is designed takes time and effort and the researcher has a right to expect the partner to make a commitment, even if it is only 'in principle', to financial support before the research is designed.

The application process

When you have agreement from a partner you might consider how to find additional funds to support the research you are undertaking. While researchers often receive funds directly from partners, the more common approach is to source extra resources from research funding bodies such as the ESRC, Marsden, or the ARC in Australia. As we have mentioned these funding bodies often ask researchers to gain financial (in kind and in cash) contributions from partners in some of the funding schemes that they offer. The amount of support that is required differs from scheme to scheme and in some cases within schemes. For example in Australia, the ARC linkage scheme requires contributions, cash and/or in-kind support depending on the nature of the partner, to demonstrate the partner's commitment to the project. In the next section of this chapter we will deal with some of the issues that relate to developing and submitting an application to one of these research grant schemes. Prior to this, there are some general principles that are worth highlighting. These general principles are intended to be useful guidelines for consideration when engaging in grant development. They are not a set of 'rules' or guarantees when applying for funding. Generally, we believe partnership research grant applications should:

- make a case for the need based on the research project's connection to practice;

- be distinctive, unique and compelling;

- outline the theoretical contribution the research will make, and to which fields;

- be achievable, sustainable through a clear scope and sequencing process;

- explain clearly the relationship with the partner;

- provide some information on the theoretical and practical benefits of the research; and

- create a clear plan for the dissemination of the research to the academic and professional community (if applicable).

From one page to ten pages

As we mentioned in Chapter 4, a one-page précis of the project is a useful first step in gaining support from a partner. This has similarities to an abstract for publication, except that it describes the outcomes and the benefits to the partner more comprehensive. *The ten-page document* is essentially a planning document that is the next step in your communication with the partner organization. After initial meetings and discussions regarding how the research fits with the partner's programmes and aims, the development of the longer, more involved document ensures all members of the team are in agreement about the what, why, how and where of the planned research. The longer document should contain a review of the relevant literature, the aims of the project, the scope of the project and any information on budgets and timelines. While this information does not necessarily go directly into the application, much of this can be transferred at a later date when you have agreement with the research partner about the more detailed aspects of the project. While some researchers involve partners in drafting the application, our practice has been to deal with the funding bodies and the application processes as they can be a complex and time consuming task for experienced researchers, let alone those who have not applied to these schemes in the past.

The ten-page document is intended to lay the foundation for the ongoing negotiations that will be necessary as you move from a general idea to a more specific and focused piece of research. Funding bodies require focused and achievable research projects. The ten-page document is the first step in clarifying and planning such a project. While these documents vary, we outline here the general ideas for what information can be included. The following subheadings provide some general categories of material that funding bodies will require as part of the application process. The kind of material required will of course, differ from funding body to funding body and this list of subheadings should be altered to suit your local context.

- Aims and background
- Significance and innovation
- Approach or methodology
- Schedule
- Dissemination of findings
- Research environment
- Partner commitment
- Personnel

The list is actually intended as a way for you to begin working on the detailed scope, methodologies, background research, and budgets to progress the project concept into a fully fledged research application. For the remainder of this chapter we explore the importance and role of each section in more detail.

Aims and background

Aims and objectives are central to research. They are both the foundation of the research idea and the main organizer of the research process. Research aims need to be achievable and if possible remarkable. Funding bodies are particularly harsh on projects that appear too big or claim too much. In addition, if your aims are succinct and expressed in a way that grabs the attention of funding bodies they will help your project stand out from the crowd of applications. Aims should describe in achievable detail the kinds of things you hope your research will accomplish. These aims must be negotiated with the partner as they will have clear ideas about what they want from the research. As we have already discussed, partner desires may not always match those of the researcher, so it is useful to spend time ensuring you have a series of joint understandings to underpin these aims.

We have also included background in this section. While aims can be, and in some places should be, differentiated from the background of the research, creating a clear link between the background and the aims will assist in developing your case for the research. The background describes why the research is crucial and timely. It explains why the partnership makes sense and provides the research funders with the information they require to be able to determine the need for the research. This need could be related to theory, practice, methodology or policy development. The way you establish the background will depend on the particular requirements of the research grant you are applying for. Recently, we submitted an application exploring the link between playwriting and literacy. In our context, literacy education is a major priority for governments, bureaucracies and schools. By creating a background that links our interests with a prevailing priority, our research contextualized itself within government policy position. So, the background should create a context for the research, describe the need for the research and give funders a succinct and direct understanding of why your research matters. It is also the case that the background is the section of the application that is often read first by assessors and is therefore your first chance to make a strong impression with the need and the aims of your research project.

Significance and innovation

The background will introduce the reader to the compelling but general need for the research. In many grant applications a separate section is provided to expand on this, offer more detail and explain how the research is significant and to whom. In education most of the projects that we propose have direct significance for those in schools, universities and other places of learning. The mistake, however, is to imagine that the significance that seems obvious to educators is obvious to grant assessors. Grant assessors come from a variety of areas, some outside education, and do not readily understand the issues and concerns significant to educators and educational researchers. The application must explain in clear terms why your research will make a difference. While the significance section should not be couched in terms that are competitive with other applications, you will obviously need to consider the claims of other grant applicants and develop a significance section that stands out.

Often coupled with the significance of the research is a consideration of the innovation of the research. This consideration requires researchers to identify the specifically innovative aspects of their project. This innovation could relate to the methodologies used, the area being researched or the nature of the research partnership. Consider similar research projects that you know of when drafting this section so that the claims you make cannot be contradicted by someone assessing this project with a detailed knowledge of the area. Claims for innovation should be made carefully as they can be easily contradicted if there is scant evidence for your claims. A weak innovation or significance claim will harm your credibility. On the other hand, a strong claim will make you distinctive against other research projects in the area. The following list outlined some of the ways you can make a claim for significance and innovation:

- Addresses an important problem

- Advances in the knowledge base

- Advances theoretical knowledge

- Innovative aims and concepts

- Methodological innovation

- National benefit

- International relevance or impact.

Depending on your particular study, it can be more effective to make a strong claim for one or two innovative elements rather than a general discussion of innovation that attempts to cover a variety of broad issues.

Approach or methodology

The approach or methodology section should provide assessors with a clear and detailed understanding of what the research process will entail and whether the methodologies you have chosen suit the needs of the research. Suiting the methodology to the project is crucial. This section should closely link with the aims so that the approach you choose meets the needs that you have identified. If your research identifies mixed methods approaches you should clearly identify which method is being used, at what point it is being used, and the outcomes you are expecting from each research strategy. It is sometimes useful to provide this visually – to include a table or a graph outlining the different research phases and the different research strategies. If the research methodology is complex then this assists the grant assessors by providing a clear outline of which strategies are being used at which time and for what.

Schedule

Grant applications should provide the assessors with a clear plan for the way the research will unfold. The nature of almost all research is that timelines are sometimes urgent and indistinct, and so it is not always clear what will happen when. It is also the case that data collection in institutions such as schools is at the mercy of pressures and timetables beyond the researcher's control. Research granting bodies and application assessors do understand this reality. Therefore, while it is understood your plan may change as the research develops, grant assessors will want to know, at least in an indicative manner, the way you think the research will proceed. This gives them a good understanding of whether the research aims you have stated are achievable within the time frames you have identified. When planning the research schedule you must make clear to research partners that timelines and schedules will change as a normal part of the research. As a general principle, you should be conservative about the time it will take to deliver on your research. Table 6.2 provides a sample delivery schedule developed from a recent research project.

Table 6.2 Research schedule

Completion Date	Item
By 5 April	International case study collaborators identified and contacted
15 May	International case studies underway
By 17 May	Publication proposals submitted. One per CI & researcher
Early June	Individual case study analysis is completed (11 weeks)
Mid-July	Publication: 1st draft completed
Mid July	Two-day publication workshop
Last week July	Two-day analysis workshop
End of Aug	2nd draft publications
Early Sept	Analysis of merged case studies (12 weeks)
Mid-Sept	One-day meeting re. research report
27 Sept	Submission of publications
4 Oct	1st draft of report
1 Nov	2nd draft of report
22 Nov	3rd draft report
29 Nov	Report ready for submission

Dissemination of research findings

Many of the international funding bodies analyse the impact of research in different ways. One of the most established ways of assessing research impact is through the amount and quality of the publications that emerge from the research. We examine research dissemination in more detail in Chapter 9, but include a brief discussion here focusing on the context of the application as many research grants require a detailed and thoughtful discussion of your dissemination strategy. When you are considering dissemination in the context of partnership research you should carefully consider the ways that the research can be communicated beyond the academic community. Assessors will be looking for evidence that you understand how to communicate the findings of your research to the professional community that you are partnering with. For instance, if your research relates to innovative teaching strategies there are obvious opportunities for you to share those findings with communities of teachers and school leaders at events such as workshops, presentation at professional conferences. This will indicate your readiness to move the knowledge you have generated beyond the academy and into the professional community that it serves. As a partnership researcher, you are most likely philosophically committed to disseminating your research in places that it will have the most benefit – to make the knowledge matter. Signalling this in the research application provides a good foundation for you to make this aspiration a reality. It also signals to the assessor that you care about making your research relevant and responsive to the needs of the sector you are researching within.

Research environment

In Chapter 4 we discussed this new criterion and the way in which is relates to how one might develop a research team. In terms of resourcing, this criterion is attempting to ensure you can deliver with the resources available to your research institution. In partnership research, your research environment also includes the resources of the partner. When you are considering the resources available to you in your budget you should discuss the research opportunities available within the partner's and the research institution's resources. Here you can also make a claim regarding how the connections forged between your and the partner's organizations can benefit the profession more broadly (for example, informing the professional development of teachers or the provision of high quality programmes for students). From a resourcing point of view, where your institution may not have the required equipment or personnel the partner organization can often make those resources available to the research. In most research grant schemes, resources can be included as research support 'in kind' for the purposes of budgeting. Crucial to this criteria is to make a strong case that you, in partnership with your partner, can deliver on the research that you have promised within the resources you have available to you. Beyond physical resources, this includes mentoring opportunities from senior researchers, dissemination support, financial management support, and any other physical resources that may be useful. Here you can include your collaborating researchers' resources as well.

Partner organization commitment and collaboration

The partner organization's involvement and commitment to the project will be assessed in most grant application processes. Assessors look for evidence that the partner is committed to the research. Often this takes the form of a cash contribution, but also in many circumstances includes an contribution in kind to the research project. Almost always, the partner commitment is determined according to the resources they are willing to contribute to the research. Having said that, there should also be evidence in this section of the application that the partner has been involved in the design and negotiation of the project and that it meets their needs as well as the needs of the researcher. Assessors are aware that projects that align well with partner needs are likely to receive high levels of support and commitment. If the partner has approached you to undertake the research it is worth signalling in this part of the application. Ordinarily, the research partner has agreed to be part of the research project that you are proposing because it fits within the stated research or strategic priorities. If this is the case, include these priorities as evidence that the research partner has identified these areas and is keen to understand them through an engagement in this research. It is worth being as specific as possible in this section, providing evidence where it is available to create a link between the partner's strategic interests and the research that you are proposing.

Personnel

The composition of your team will be one of the most crucial factors in the success of your project. It will also be a key criterion for those assessing your project. As we discussed earlier when you are developing your team you should consider the various contributions the members can make to the research and the extent to which the team has established a research track record. While all members of your team do not have to be experienced researchers with a sustained research track record, it is important to make the case that you have sufficient human resources and experience to deliver the aims of the project. In some research grants there is a preference for including early career researchers on the team to provide opportunities for research mentoring and training. Normally this section of a grant application requires a list of publications, research track record, and other evidence of research output from the research team. There is also usually a section that requires an explication of the particular roles of the members of the research team – essentially identifying who will be doing what in the research. This should link to the methods and approaches section of the application as you will need to match the researcher to the research task. For instance, if you have a qualitative researcher on your team you will need to identify them clearly in the design and the delivery of the qualitative aspects of the research so that assessors understand the role in the research and can see the link between their experience and the expected outcomes of the research. Research teams can use this section to confirm and outline the governance of the research. This lets assessors (and the research team) know succinctly where the lines of supervision are and who will be accountable for what aspects of the research. This section should also outline how personnel from the partner organization will be integrated within the research project. Assessors are looking for clear evidence that there are structures for the efficient delivery of the research aims, that the partner and research team have the capacity to work in an efficient and mutually beneficial way, and that those in charge have experience to deliver research at the scale they are requesting.

Conclusions

Funding research has been a preoccupation for researchers for as long as there has been research to do. It can be one of the most frustrating and difficult aspects of a researcher's job. There is, however, little choice for those of us who have big research ideas but to find avenues for funding. The strategies we have detailed in this chapter will hopefully provide you with some ideas about how to source research funds and then how to apply for them. As always, research will be funded on the basis of how well you understand your audience and how effectively you can connect with their needs and communicate your ideas. Applying for research to granting bodies is difficult. There are, however, many benefits to working in this way. It allows you to create research that would not otherwise be possible.

Our last piece of advice is not to be discouraged. In our experience, many good research applications have had to be submitted three or four times before they are successful. It is common to be knocked back on an application because it did not fit the particular requirements of that funding body or because the competition for funding in a particular round was unusually fierce. Resilience is required to take the criticisms that come with rejection, but if you can learn from these criticisms and discern the beneficial critique from the pointless, you will be able to develop more robust and effective research proposals. In the next chapter, we deal with that terrifying moment when you actually are successful in your research grant application. We say terrifying because although having the opportunity to actually implement research grants is a much sought after opportunity, delivery of partnership research can be as challenging as it is rewarding.

Key messages from the chapter

- Early career researchers in education often find it beneficial to generate their own research project that is funded from within their own resources. If the project is closely tied to the professional role of the researcher (as a teacher etc.) it can reduce the costs of the research.

- Think carefully about whether you require external funding for your projects. Application processes are time-consuming and can be unproductive. Grant applications routinely take weeks of development that could be better used actually doing research if external funding is not required.

- Funding can assist partnership projects that cannot be managed solely with the capacities that you and your partners have at their disposal. Funded grants are also useful for career progression.

- Large government granting organizations often identify impact is a key criteria for funding partnership research. This is a good match for researchers interested in making change possible through their research.

- When looking for funding from non-government organizations it is often possible to fit the agenda of the organization by amplifying and reshaping your original idea to fit the needs of the funder. Successful partnership researchers become skilled at finding connections between their research interests and ideas and the external priorities of potential funders.

- Generally, we believe partnership research grant applications should be distinctive, unique and compelling, be achievable, not be repetitive in any way, explain clearly the relationship with the partner, provide some information on the theoretical and practical benefits of the research, create a clear plan for the dissemination of the research to the academic and professional community.

CHAPTER SEVEN

Delivering partnership research

We have spent a substantial amount of time in this book talking about planning for partnership research. We have done this because in partnership research, the planning phases are crucial – it is where networks are made, research sites are formed, and roles and responsibilities are delineated. However, once planned and resourced, the research needs to be delivered. When working in partnerships in education, there are particular benefits and challenges in the implementation and delivery of research. This chapter begins the discussion about how partnership research can be delivered in a timely and efficient manner that supports the needs of the partner and the needs of the researcher. There are significant overlaps between the planning, implementation and the publication processes. We have called this chapter 'Delivering Partnership Research' to indicate that planning, implementation and publication overlaps significantly throughout the course of any research project.

Metaphorically, the research process is much like the building process. Detailed plans need to be submitted, and then the long process of application and approval is endured. The real excitement begins, however, when construction starts. Considered metaphorically, research begins with the breaking of the ground. The research team is established, and at last the plans you have submitted need to be converted into practical research tasks. This can be daunting, because oftentimes the plans put forward in the application, when the research project existed as an abstract concept, may seem difficult to deliver when the research becomes a practical reality. Added to this difficulty, funding bodies often fail to fund the research at requested levels. Therefore, before 'ground is broken', to continue the analogy, you will need to reassess the aims and the scope of the research with your partners. This chapter explores the practical research tasks often involved in partnership research. It will cover fieldwork in research sites, how to ensure the metaphorical 'foundations' of the building are solid, and what to do if things start to go awry. Like any construction process, there can be setbacks that are outside your control; however, with realistic expectations and a willingness by all parties to be flexible, good, solid and relevant research is not only possible, but likely.

Organizing your team

An issue that can make the research tasks seem overwhelming is when there are personnel changes made to the research team or partner organization. People move on for various reasons – a change in position, changes to personal circumstances and so on. The long application process of many research projects make personnel changes a reality of partnership research. In a project we were recently involved with almost half the research team had left the project because of retirement, and changes in the circumstances before the research was half way through. It is essential to have a plan for managing changes to the research team, particularly if the person or people moving on are central to, or champions for, the research project. In these circumstances, our approach has been to meet with our collaborating researchers, identify the gaps, assess to what extent the research has changed due to the level of funding provided and decide whether more or different staff at required to deliver the research aims.

Many research projects identify a research manager in their application. If you receive funding a for research manager you will most likely need to advertise this position. We have created a sample advertisement to provide some sense of the requirements of the role below.

Theatre Education Research International is a new centre for Research and Development that will support theatre and theatre education internationally. This is a joint initiative of several national government arts agencies and research councils.

The Research Manager is a pivotal position for this initiative, and the successful candidate will be responsible for managing a variety of research and development activities to support the growth and sustainability of theatre and theatre education research.

We therefore seek an individual with demonstrated experience and expertise in theatre and theatre education research, who is able to design and manage large-scale research projects across multiple settings and in diverse communities. In addition, the appointee will work closely with researchers in various international universities and with national government arts agencies and research councils to build large-scale initiatives to support the growth and development of theatre and theatre education.

Application procedures and a full position description with detailed selection criteria are available on request.

In addition many research projects also include PhD students to support the research training aims of the project. Often these positions also need to be advertised. There are many benefits of including PhD students in your research team, it is a reciprocal relationship that has benefits for both the research team and the student, as they both benefit from each other's work and expertise. Further, it is of benefit to the education research field more generally as it provides mentoring and networking for those training to be researchers. It may be worth considering recruiting for these positions as you are developing your plans, submitting your ethics proposals, and negotiating contractual matters. In our experience recruiting doctoral students and research management personnel can take three to four months or longer. This should be accounted for in the timeline and planning of your research project.

Meetings

Meetings are a necessary aspect of partnership research. When well-planned and resourced, meetings can be the most effective way to communicate with the team, plan the research, analyse data and organize data reporting. Unplanned meetings, however, can be colossal time-wasters – lengthy and wordy without any purpose. When you are planning to meet ensure that you have the objectives of the meeting foremost in your mind. Freeform meetings that abound in universities are not usually productive when it comes to partnership research. Research team meetings do not have to be weekly or biweekly but they should instead meet the needs of the research project. It is best to hold these meetings when there is something to organize or something to resolve and not simply for the sake of meeting. Incidental communication can often be done through email or a project wiki. The exception to this rule is meetings with the partner organizations. Researcher–partner meetings should be held on a regular basis to update the partner on the progress of the research. In our experience, projects that do not use regular meetings to update the partners tend to become remote from the partner and this can lead to deterioration in the relationship between the partners and the researchers. Timely, ordered and directed meetings avoid the likelihood of an irreparable breakdown in relationships between the partners and the researchers. While there will be differences of opinion and on occasion robust exchanges, these regular meetings will at least ensure that the partner stays 'in the loop'.

On our projects, we usually offer a meeting with the partners every two months. This offer is not always taken up, but it is always made. These meetings usually keep the partner in the loop about the progress of the research and also offer an opportunity for the partner to continue considering the research as part of their future plans. It also keeps the research team at the forefront of the partners thinking. Most partners in research have many other priorities apart from the research project that they are engaged with and so these meetings continue to give the project priority for the partner organization. It is a useful way of underscoring the relevance of the research and identifying how the internal politics of the partner organization might be changing, and how this will potentially affect the research and researchers.

Communication

There are no perfect ways to organize communication strategies amongst teams in partnership research. Some teams will require meetings weekly in the intensive phases of the research, while other projects can survive with meetings once or twice a year. If you have a team which is geographically dispersed it may be worth considering the development of a system of shared calendars, and a project wiki so that information can be updated and any issues that arise can be addressed. Some researchers have shared online workspaces where documents and other research resources can be stored. These shared workspaces are invaluable if your team is disbursed or if there are several research sites. Being able to access a central repository of information ensures that the team is not reinventing resources and wasting time duplicating tasks. Shared spaces in the 'cloud', such as Dropbox, also allow for some data sharing and make drafting processes more streamlined. As a rule time spent developing communication logistics will allow for more efficient processes and hopefully lead to less frustration amongst team members.

Advisory groups: Supporting the planning and delivery of the research

As discussed earlier it is often useful to include a research advisory group to assist in the application and implementation of your research project. An advisory group provides a formal way for you to include those who cannot be named as chief investigators or take a formal research role but who are helpful for the development and delivery of your research. This advisory group gives the project depth of personnel beyond the researchers and the partners and provides funders with confidence that your research has sufficient support to ensure it sufficient and ethical progress. Typically, this group has members of your broader academic community, industry professionals that have an interest in the research, other stakeholder groups and research support staff from your institution. While we have not used an advisory group in a project more than once or twice a year, their association with the research has been useful for giving advice and support through all phases of the project. In addition, they have provided sage advice about how to manage some of the more difficult challenges the project faced. We typically identify and name this advisory group in our applications and suggest that we will meet virtually or face-to-face half yearly or at least yearly. Your partner should also be involved in advisory board meetings as this provides them with a deeper insight into the research issues and provides valuable networking opportunities.

The first meeting with your partner

One of the first steps we take when 'breaking the ground for the research' is to meet again with the the partner organization to ensure the aims and anticipated outcomes of the research remain the same as they were when the application was submitted. Ordinarily, partners and research institutions will need to sign a contract of agreement supplied by the granting organization to formalize the relationship between the researchers and the partner. This provides a good pretext for discussions about expectations of the research. It also provides an opportunity for issues such as intellectual property, research roles and responsibilities, publication outcomes and other expectations to be discussed. Approaching this meeting with details of timelines and research deliverables will reinforce for the partner your ability to deliver on your plans. This is also an opportunity to offer extra support for your partner through professional development, research advice or consultancy. In our experience, partnerships run on goodwill and offering extra support to partners can deepen and enhance your rapport with them. It also signals to them that you are interested in a long-term relationship that features reciprocity between researchers and partners. In a recent 'first meeting' while discussing the logistical issues of the research, the partner mentioned that they were seeking, as part of a different programme, some professional development for their staff. We offered to assist the partner by running this training for them, which allowed the partner to see that we were serious about capacity building in the organization and allowed us to become involved in the broader organization. The first meeting is crucial for setting the tone of the relationship that is to come. If you can signal that even though you now have the funds to undertake the research you are still keen to support the development and growth of the partner organization it is likely to create an environment of trust. Beyond the building of a rapport, at the end of this meeting you should have a clear idea of your partner's expectations and they should have a clear understanding of your capacity and willingness to deliver in a timely but realistic way.

Ethics

In most research projects ethics approvals will be required before you enter the field and collect data. Some applications require ethical clearances prior to submission but in most jurisdictions ethics applications are completed when the grant is approved for funding. Much of the detailed information in your research application and other documents will be useful in the preparation of ethics applications and subsequent clearances. You should discuss with your partner at the initial meeting their procedures and approaches to ethics. It may be that you need to submit ethics applications to several separate bodies. All of these applications take time so you should budget for a delay while you submit and respond to any ethics issues that arise. It is not unusual for ethics applications to take six to nine months to be approved, especially in situations where your research deals with sensitive issues or sensitive populations. This should not be seen as wasted time, you can spend time putting together and consolidating your team, updating your understanding of the theoretical background of your research field, and working on the various timetables for implementation of your research. You can also begin the detailed practical planning process for the research organizing the first meeting with your partner.

Although ethics applications can seem like they are irritating and time consuming they are a process that can build trust between your partner and the research team. In education we are faced with some especially challenging ethical dilemmas, as our research participants are often young children. If you are undertaking research within a school that involves students or teachers you may need to obtain ethical clearances from a department of education. This has a dual purpose. It lets your system (university, school, etc.) know what you are doing and covers you ethically. Your research institution will be able to provide support for you in the development of this application but we thought it might be worthwhile outlining some of the key principles that guide the preparation of ethics applications in partnership research. The first area that partnership researchers will need to deal with is anonymity and confidentiality.

Anonymity and confidentiality

Researchers take different views about anonymity in educational research. Punch argues, 'there is strong feeling among most fieldworkers that settings and respondents should not be identifiable in print and that they should not suffer harm or embarrassment as a consequence of research' (Punch 1994: p. 93). Other researchers such as Shulman (1990: p. 11) take a very different view claiming that participants' voices should be recognized. However, she also points to the consequences and implications of revealing participant identities that may single them out for ridicule and oppression. Her study into the attitudes of teachers in classrooms left her participants potentially vulnerable as 'teachers rarely leave the scene [of the research]. They must bear the burden of their written words, for they remain participants long after they complete their roles' (Shulman 1990: p. 14).

Anonymity can empower research participants to speak out about their experience of other teachers, colleagues or supervisors in ways that would be impossible if they were identified publicly (Shulman 1990: p. 11). Pseudonyms are useful for the research participants, participants' schools and any other person who could be used to identify the research participants. Broad geographical areas can be used to identify and contextualize the location of the research participants. Our advice is to take the safe course and make your participants anonymous. Your participants may decide that they would like to associate themselves with the research but this decision should not be yours. Having said that, in situations where partners and/or different participants have differing views about anonymity, then you may need to make a clear decision regarding your reporting of the data. This decision should be made in ways that align with the ethics requirements of your organization and must be communicated with all members of the team, the partners and the participants. In a study undertaken in a school recently, we were faced with this issue when, after collecting data and assuring our teacher participants it would be anonymous, the school leaders decided they would like to be named in the research as it assisted with their annual reporting. The partners were also keen to have participants named. This decision caused distrust amongst the participants and we made the decision that, because the participants were assured anonymity when they participated in the original data collection, we would maintain this for all participants, at all levels of the study. Had the schools or partner organization made their preferences known prior to data collection, this could have been handled more effectively.

Transparency: Informed consent and deception

In research that seeks to include participants as partners in the research, informed consent is crucial. It provides a transparency for the motives of the research that cannot be assured if there is deception in the research process. For instance, if you are exploring if history learning promotes participation in democratic processes the following description would appear in your participant information sheet:

> This study will explore whether history learning processes encourage participation in democratic learning. In this study we will interview you about your participation in politics and your engagement with democratic processes such as voting. At no time during this process will you be asked to reveal your political views.

This clearly and in plain English outlines the intent of the study and the expectations of the participants. It also lets the research participants know what they will not be asked to reveal. We cannot think of a reason that participants in partnership research (or any kind of educational research) should be deceived. We realize there are different views on covert research. In research that includes children, as much education research does, we believe researchers should pay close attention to the ethical implications of research that uses these techniques. Transparent research approaches keep trust and faith with those we are working with and addresses the inherent power imbalance between the researcher and the researched. As you are finalizing your ethics application, your thoughts should turn to establishing the other protocols that will enable effective research.

Establishing protocols

When you receive ethics approval the next phase of the research will require you and your collaborating researchers to create detailed and realistic protocols for conducting the research. By protocols we mean the shared understanding between the researchers, the partners and the participants about the way the research will be conducted. In other words, what can everyone expect to happen and when? Much of the hard work of protocol development will be done in the ethics proposal as most applications require a detailed description of the what, how, who and when of the project. You will need, however, to discuss with your team how to work with educational institutions. For partnership researchers in education, protocols are critically important as many educational researchers work directly with students in classrooms, we will discuss protocols as they relate directly to children in schools in the sections below.

Dealing with the financials

Many academics do not have the skills to deal with the complex financial arrangements that are part and parcel of research management. Many application processes include a budget template that reflects the various financial rules related to each specific grant scheme. When it comes to the financial management of research we have found it useful to develop a spreadsheet of all the costs related to the research as a first step. This document allows us to gain advice from those who have a more detailed knowledge in this area. Often partnership research projects have detailed and complex financial arrangements that need to be monitored regularly to ensure the project stays on time and on budget. When considering the composition of your team, it is worth considering recruiting a team member with financial management expertise to support you in this aspect of the project. It may be that the partner organization has some resources that they can contribute to support your financial planning and management as well.

When research projects are funded at lower levels than had been requested in the application, there is a requirement to redraw and rethink the budget. If you have received a cut to your budget you will need to consider reducing the scope of your research project. Funding bodies understand that this is a necessary part of controlling the scope and costs of your project. If the application is not funded in full then funding organizations usually do not expect the research project to align exactly with the application description. Therefore, you should not attempt to undertake the research you proposed in the application with less funding than is required – this will not only be a strain on you and your partner organization's resources, it will most probably result in sub-standard research. If the application process has been long, or the study is longitudinal in nature, you will also need to consider the likely effects of costs rising due to inflation. Personnel costs are particularly susceptible to shifts and a generous yearly increase should be budgeted as part of your planning processes.

Most research institutions have budgetry processes and will provide advice for researchers. These resources can be very useful if you do not have the skills within your team to manage the financial aspects of your research. Even if you do have these skills each institution is likely to have their own particular protocols. Regular meetings and contact with financial and other administration staff will provide the advice you need and allow you to concentrate on delivering the outcomes of the research.

Into the field: School-based partnership research

Schools are places that run on timetables and schedules. Shared understandings of the ways researchers will access and conduct themselves in schools are essential to educational institutions providing access and allowing trust to develop with the researchers. If you have a research project that relies on schools for data collection you will need to make contact with schools early and in some cases you will find it difficult to gain access. It seems in the last decade that schools had been bombarded with requests for data collection, and you may find schools less than eager to engage in your research project. In the same way as you may have used your networks to initiate contact with your partner organization, school contacts are a precious commodity for a school-based partnership researcher. If you have someone who works within the school who can coordinate the relationship with the school, this should lead to a smooth a relationship in that research site. In some school-based research, teachers are paid as research assistants to act as the coordinator of this research. In our projects we have not been funded at levels that would allow this, but it does seem like a good idea given the time and effort teachers need to expend supporting research in schools. Some schools appoint a research coordinator to cope with the abundant requests they receive. Often schools will be excited by research that aligns with their own needs, and so it is worth investigating which school sites might benefit from the research you are undertaking. Many schools are required to meet policy standards or goals to maintain their funding (such as community engagement or improvement in literacy) and therefore will be seeking research programmes that can serve as evidence for their work in this area. One of the best models we've seen is an approach with schools that includes teachers in the research as PhD students or masters students and provides them with an opportunity to develop and extend their research capacities as part of the research team. Of course, issues related to conflicts of interest need to be addressed if you are considering this model for school-based research.

Once the protocols have been established and participants have been recruited, it is time to enter the field. This can be a simultaneously exhilarating and daunting prospect for many researchers. Schools, unlike laboratories are not set up primarily for research, they are designed and run for the education and welfare of their students. Researchers in schools need to keep a realistic perspective of their place in the school at all times. As a researcher you are there at the school's discretion. When entering the school, researchers should be aware of the protocols that apply to visitors. In most cases, the principal should be advised of your arrival at the school and you are usually required to sign documentation that relates to your behaviour and conduct in the school. There are also likely to be protocols around child protection that require you to make disclosures about any criminal history or child related offences. This is usually dealt with at the ethics proposal stage but if you are leading a research team it is crucial to obtain clearances for all of your researchers before any researcher enters a school. In many jurisdictions child protection training is available and you should avail yourself of this training if you are not familiar with the regulations and expectations in this area.

Schools are sometimes unpredictable places for researchers. Plans that you have made to meet a teacher or a group of students are routinely derailed by emergencies, changes in schedule and misunderstandings. Recently, when collecting data for a partnership research project in a high school, we arrived to find the teacher had gone on an excursion unexpectedly to replace a colleague who had phoned in sick. Countless times school visits have been rescheduled, students have been unavailable (because they are absent, on detention, doing an exam, rehearsing a play, the list goes on). This is frustrating, it delays the research and may mean the researchers spend hours travelling to find they cannot collect any data. Unfortunately for researchers this is the nature of education research sites. Teachers often work in very stressful situations and if research exacerbates the stress researchers will see deterioration in any goodwill that they had built up. The simplest way to avoid this is to attempt to be as unobtrusive as possible and fit as much as possible with the needs of the school. There are obviously ways researchers in schools provide a service to schools; however, many researchers in the past have made things difficult for themselves and other researchers by expecting schools to work around them. In essence, the best approach is to understand your context and negotiate with the school every step of the way so that your visit is a positive experience for you and the school. Long-term relationships are built with schools when researchers are sensitive to the needs and supportive of their protocols. You can build productive relationships with schools that will be mutually beneficial if your first approach respects the school and you understand your place within it. On a practical note, it is always worth providing your participants with your mobile phone number so they can call you if there is a change to established plans.

Managing the teams

We discussed earlier establishing the team of researchers, partners, participants and advisory board members. Beyond this initial development, long-term management of research teams has its challenges. Over the course of any substantial research your team will change. Sometimes the changes are minor such as a team member needing to take time off due to illness, and sometimes they are quite major such as the retirement of the researcher. In the course of our partnership research career we have faced both situations. Even if you have a small team of researchers it is likely that you will need to manage change throughout the life of the research project. One of the best ways to make your project resilient and sustainable is to share the necessary knowledge, organizational intricacies and theoretical understandings in the research team. Regular meetings are one way to develop an understanding between team members and an *esprit de corps* for the research. Regular meetings can be challenging when researchers are geographically scattered. One strategy for teams that struggle to maintain regular meetings is to have regular (for example, bi-yearly) workshops where all of the team meets and works through some of the research issues arising. These meetings are usually most productive when they are used to work on something tangible – such as coding or analysing data. This allows the researchers to develop a shared knowledge and understanding of the processes and approaches required in the analysis of the data emerging from the project. These kinds of meetings also allow researchers to discuss issues of concern to them; while these may be contentious, it allows everybody a say in the running of the research. These meetings can then be complemented by regular Skype and teleconference meetings with the whole team and at times between researchers working on sub-projects within the larger project. We are not claiming that this is a perfect way to do large partnership research. These meetings can, however, provide a forum for everyone to exchange views and to discuss issues in the implementation of the research.

In the design of your research you should provide sufficient space for team members to express their ideas, and become aware of the knowledge that is being generated through the processes and the content of the research. If there are changes in your research personnel this shared understanding will allow others to fill those gaps if you need to recruit new researchers.

Delivering quality research

If you are leading your research team you will need to continuously monitor the quality of the research you are undertaking. Perhaps the first step is to measure the outputs of your research against the aims you have stated in your application. One useful strategy is to a standing item on the agenda of your regular meeting with your research partner that addresses how the research aims are being delivered. Another approach is to detail the deliverables and report to your partner against your timeline.

Your advisory group has a role to play in supporting quality research as well. In some research projects we have asked a member of the advisory group to act as research auditor on the research project. This quality assurance strategy allows someone familiar with the research, but at a distance from it, to provide advice on the operation of the research. This role is often described as a 'critical friend'. Costa and Kallick (1993) describe the role this way. A critical friend is 'a trusted person who asks provocative questions, provides data to be examined through another lens, and offers critique of a person's work as a friend'. Their role is to examine the aims and deliverables of the research and provide critique on them. The other aspect of their role is to suggest possible solutions for the critiques they provide. In our experience, it is better to receive a little bit of 'tough love' early on in the research and fix emerging problems rather than to wait until the research is complete and deal with problems in retrospect. Critical friends can also ensure credibility and support the validation processes of the research.

Validity and credibility

Validity reflects the extent to which your research is 'sound, cogent, well grounded, justifiable or logically correct' (Schwandt 2001). If research is credible it should be trustworthy (Schwandt, 2001) in that it truly reflects the authentic voice of the participants and resonates with others who will be engaged by the research. Many partnership research methodologies seek to remove the traditional researcher and researched status. This partnership can be maintained by ensuring the research participants feel that the research undertaken with them reflects what they feel they wanted to communicate as part of the research. Giving research participants an opportunity to respond to their contribution ensures the reliability and the credibility of the research. Research participants may ask for changes to the research and even though the researcher may disagree with these sentiments, they have the right to be represented in ways that they feel are valid. Naturally, this requires negotiation on the part of the researcher and the participants but the voice and wishes of the participants are central to the validity of the research. The credibility of the research lies in the authenticity and clarity of the research participants' voices and their transferability, creating knowledge that leads to a deeper understanding of the research question. There are many useful measures of credibility but in our experience one of the most useful is crystallization.

Crystallization

Crystallization and triangulation, along with the authenticity of research participants' voices, is a key strategy to develop the reliability of qualitative research. Triangulation is the use of a variety of data sources in a study (Janesick 1994: p. 214). It is a useful term but does suggest limitation. We prefer the crystallization method as it has greater scope to validate the data. Richardson argues that the 'central image for "validity" for post–modernist texts is not the triangle – a rigid, fixed, two dimensional object. Rather, the central image is the crystal, which combines symmetry and substance with an infinite variety of shapes, substances, transmutations, multidimensionalities, and angles of approach. Crystals grow, change, alter but are not amorphous' (Richardson 1994: p. 522).

Crystallization seems more able to describe the multitude of approaches researchers use to validate the research data. The process also reflects the possibility of several reflections from the same source, in other words several interpretations from the one interview, narrative or case study. The researcher's interpretations may be only one of the many interpretations possible. For instance, if your study examined teachers' experience of the classroom through narratives you might use several methods of validation for the narratives. Firstly, the teachers in the study could validate the narratives (one facet of the crystal). The teachers might then be asked to read the narratives and respond by indicating whether the narratives reflected their experience. At any point they could negotiate changes and make additions to the narratives. This validation allows the authentic voices of participants to emerge and ensures the researchers style or voice does not overwhelm their voices. Another facet of this crystallization process might be to engage critical friends or other researchers in the data analysis to suggest any alternative interpretations of the data.

Leaving the field

One of the most difficult challenges for partnership research is to know when to stop collecting data and leave the research field. If the research is planned effectively, there will usually be a nominated point at which data collection stops. This may be dictated by time or by data. Time-dictated data collection may involve participants in one particular year of schooling or throughout one unit of work. Data-dictated collection usually continues until the required data is obtained, such as a particular number of interviews, observations or work samples. Time frames obviously change, but it is worth maintaining accurate timelines or details of necessary data collected, so that your team understands when the research-collection phase concludes. In your regular meetings with your partner you should also notify them of changes to be timelines and let them know when your data collection will finish. For many projects, analysis is not possible until data collection has been completed. Inexperienced researchers may feel they should continue collecting data in the fear that they will not find enough in the data they have. In our experience a research project of any length will collect a large amount of data (usually more than one realizes!). If you have followed your plans you should resist the temptation to collect more than is needed and save extra collection of data for a new project.

Analysing the data

When you have left the field it is time to begin data analysis. This also provides a good point to convene meetings of your research team, advisory group, and with the partner. These meetings allow you to update them on the process of data collection, any problems that have been encountered, and your plans for analysis and dissemination of the data. At this point you may also need to consider recruiting new members to your team or advisory board depending on what is emerging from the data. In your planning you should consider the kinds of skill sets each phase of the research requires and budget for those requirements. This phase of the research requires different approaches and different skills from the planning and collection phases of the research. The composition of your team, the budget, and time taken for analysis, will need to be considered when you enter this phase of the research. Making the data available to your researchers through web-based technology can assist efficient analysis in large teams. In a recent project all of the data from all of the sites were centralized on one research institutions' database which allowed researchers nationally and internationally access to the data for use in analysis and publication. This made collaboration between geographically disparate research teams in the analysis process possible. Large-scale research projects have been able to expand their capacity as these technologies have become more powerful, accessible & stable. This stability, however, should not be taken for granted. If the data is housed in one place, the research team should ensure that there are several backups in several places to avoid data loss which is potentially debilitating for partnership researchers.

Conclusions

When the data collection and analysis processes are over it is time to consider the next phase of the research. At this stage the research team should be considering their next application arising from some of the unanswered questions and emergent themes of the current research. While it is often exhausting to even consider the next project, doing so before the last project concludes will maintain momentum and allow the team to consider the question of future directions for research in the area. This is also the time to ask your partner about their emerging research priorities. For many partners, reliable and productive research teams and the intellectual property that has been developed as part of the research are an asset. Maintaining this relationship may well provide the impetus for exploring new issues of relevance to the partner. If your current partner is not ready to commit again to research this may be the time to consider new partners. The research partnership you are about to conclude should provide ample evidence of your ability to deliver complex partnership research and will be a useful way to open conversations with potential partners.

Key messages from the chapter

- After long application processes, partnership research teams often need to be reconfigured because of personnel changes made to the research team or partner organization. These changes are natural and normal but the reconfiguration should be managed in consultation with the partner organization and in some cases the funding body.

- Research meetings should be well-planned and will most likely address the planning, data analysis and data reporting. Unplanned meetings can be colossal time-wasters and will sap the morale from a research team.

- All teams are different in their communication needs. The administration and organization of teams can benefit from of a system of shared calendars and project wikis so that information can be updated and any issues that arise can be addressed. Being able to access a central repository of information ensures that the team is not reinventing resources and wasting time duplicating tasks.

- The first few meetings with your research partners should develop a set of shared expectations including timelines and research deliverables, and give the research team the opportunity to reassure the partner that you can deliver on your plans. This meeting also provides an opportunity to offer extra support for your partner through professional development, research advice or consultancy.

- If you have a research project that relies on schools for data collection you will need to make contact with schools early to arrange access to the research site and discuss school logistics and protocols.

- If you are leading your research team you will need to continuously monitor the quality of the research as it progresses. One of the key benchmarking approaches is to measure what you have achieved in the actual research against what you said you would achieve in the application.

CHAPTER EIGHT

Methods for partnership research

For all the discussion around the organization and particulars of research, a research project is only as good as the methods it employs. Methods and methodologies are at the heart of any research and deciding which methods best suit which research is key to a successful research project. There are countless volumes, journals, conferences and courses dedicated to helping researchers in education understand research methods. Many of these volumes include caveats about their lack of ability to cover the entire field of research methods; the field, particularly in qualitative methods, is just too broad and complex to represent in just one volume. As a result, we are not attempting to provide in depth information about research methods in this chapter. Rather, we will discuss the philosophical differences between methods, the ways in which the choice of methodology influences project design, and provide some information about a few grass-roots, mixed-methods approaches that we feel provide opportunities for partnership research in education (particularly work in schools). Central to our discussion and the choices of these methodologies is the idea of the 'teacher-researcher' (Kincheloe 2003; Goswami and Stillman 1987). The premise of this book is that research in education serves particular purposes and audiences, and to make knowledge matter in education, research must attend to the complex relationship between teaching practice, school leadership and public policy. Hargreaves claims that because of this complex relationship, decisions in education are not always based on evidence alone and that

> there are many different kinds of research directed at answering different kinds of questions; there are many different kinds of policy and ways of forming or implementing policy; there are significant differences between policy and practice. In consequence, there is no single model that applies to all cases in every circumstance and for all time, nor could there ever be one. (Hargreaves 1999: p. 244)

There is an enduring belief that there is a 'gap' between educational theory and practice – and that teachers and educational researchers should reconcile the differences between theorizing in a complex field of human activity such as education and working in it (Kelly 2008). This reconciliation does not necessarily come easily, the theory and practice of education are not only seen as two distinct bodies of knowledge, but as two *contrasting* kinds of knowledge, inhabiting opposite ends of an epistemological continuum – not just different, they are opposed (Freebody, P. and Freebody, K. 2010).

This chapter is therefore concerned with methodologies that attempt to reconcile this uneasy relationship between educational theory and practice. The discussion is divided into three main sections: quantitative methods, qualitative methods and grass-roots approaches, including design-based research, action research and arts-informed inquiry. The division of the chapter into these sections provides a relatively easy path through the explanation of methods. In reality, the divisions between these 'types' of research can be messier and more arbitrary. There has, in the past, been a strong debate between positivist and interpretive paradigms of research; however, there is an emerging 'tradition' in research that merges qualitative and quantitative methods (Newby 2010: p. 92). Throughout the chapter, we acknowledge our inability to effectively cover the field by making suggestions about further reading for those looking for a more detailed understanding of a particular methodology.

Quantitative methods

Quantitative research methods emerge from the philosophical principle of positivism. This 'guiding principle' (Newby 2010: p. 94) is the belief that truth can only be discovered through verifiable facts – that we only know what we can prove through data. Philosophically, therefore, quantitative research is aligned with the belief that reality is observable and measurable. Quantitative research is concerned with developing and testing theory and therefore research questions in quantitative research are specific hypotheses which are then tested to establish whether the theses and theory are evidenced by the data. Central to research in this paradigm is an understanding of cause and effect, and the concept of proof. This is done in a way that is considered detached from the researcher; 'the quantitative researcher views reality as "objective", "out there" independent of the researcher' (Creswell 1994: p. 4).

From a practical perspective, quantitative research involves collecting numerical data and analysing it using statistical procedures (Newby 2010). As a result, there are relatively strict procedures and a finite number of processes and decisions on the part of the researcher (this is not to say that important decisions do not need to be made). In the past quantitative research has claimed more objectivity but as Heisenberg argues, there are choices made in all research methodologies:

This ... emphasizes a subjective element in the description of atomic events, since the measuring device has been constructed by the observer, and we have to remember that what we observe is not nature in itself but nature exposed to our method of questioning. (Heisenberg 1955: p. 28)

Generally, there are two approaches within the quantitative paradigm:

1 survey studies, including questionnaires and structured interviews; and

2 experiments, including true and quasi experiments.

These two approaches, while both underpinned by the principle of positivism, have different purposes and effects. Surveys gather data, sometimes longitudinally, to generalize from a research sample to a wider population (Creswell 1994). In surveys, data is usually collected from participants once, and is used to establish descriptions of the world. Experiments test theories through action. Data is collected from participants at least twice (usually before and after an experiment) and findings aim to establish causality. Both approaches have specific design, planning, data collection and statistical analyses associated with them. This chapter is not able (or intended) to provide in-depth information about the methods associated with quantitative research, but for an excellent overview of surveys and experiments we suggest *Quantitative Research in Education: A Primer* (Hoy 2010) or, for a range of papers and examples, the *International Journal of Quantitative Research in Education*.

Central to the philosophy and practice of quantitative research is that it is able to be replicated. When the 'same' studies are repeated in differing circumstances, a deeper understanding of the phenomenon is obtained and 'statements about the world have general applicability' (Newby 2010: p. 95). This makes quantitative research in education powerful. It is able to handle large amounts of data, often resulting in research that is large-scale and/or longitudinal. The strict procedures required to undertake quantitative research allow it to be interpreted by those outside of the field of education (such as politicians and journalists), and help to make the research convincing and defensible to policymakers. That is not to say, however, that for research in education to matter it should be placed in the quantitative paradigm. Nor does it mean that, because the research is powerful it should be the 'go to' methodology for educational researchers. There have been cases where the 'power of numbers' have been used (or even misused) by those outside of the profession to meet their own needs. This is particularly true in some political debates where one set of quantitative data is used to argue diametrically opposed points. There is a concern that the 'simplicity' of the number does not allow for complex interpretive understandings about the nature of what is researched – the 'why' and 'how', rather than the 'what' and 'how many'. Therefore, although there are many 'truths' in education that can be understood through quantitative research, there are also many studies in education that are better understood through more constructivist or interpretive approaches.

Qualitative methods

Qualitative research has had a 'distinguished place in the human disciplines' since the 1920s and 1930s (Denzin and Lincoln 1994: p. 1). Unlike quantitative research, qualitative methods do not have strict procedures but are concerned with diverse ways of finding, and understanding truth. The growth and development of qualitative research recognized a need for more flexible and naturalistic research methods (Eisner 1978: p. 202). Indeed Bruner (1990: p. 130) argues that 'neither the empiricist's tested knowledge nor the rationalist's self-evident truths describe the ground on which ordinary people go about making sense of their experiences'. Qualitative research, then, is concerned with delving into the complexity of human experience.

In partnership research in education qualitative methodologies are well suited to exploring the messiness of educational practice. Elliot Eisner argues that in exploring the complexities of educational research there is little to be gained in reducing the 'human mind to a single score'. Conversely the qualitative method attempts to 'adumbrate its complexities, its potential, and its idiosyncrasies' (Eisner 1978: p. 201). In essence partnership research often explores questions that are best suited to qualitative methods Eisner defines qualitative methodology in the following ways:

> By qualitative inquiry I mean that form of inquiry that seeks the creation of qualities that are expressively patterned, that seeks the explication of wholes as the primary aim, that emphasizes the study of configurations rather than isolated entities, that regards expressive narratives and visuals as appropriate vehicles for communication. (Eisner 1978: p. 198)

Eisner's definition identifies several key elements pertinent for partnership research. His identification of the 'creation of qualities that are expressively patterned' (Eisner 1978: p. 198) foreshadows the kinds of themes that emerge from many partnership research projects. Eisner's contention is that teachers' experiences, although individual, contain within them patterns that may inform the discussion of teacher professional development. In this example, qualitative approaches may be favoured as they allow for complexity to be represented. Essentially, the choice of methodology is derived from the research question. Questions that require the researcher to logically deduce meaning from evidence are generally suited to quantitative methods, whereas questions that require researchers to 'assemble the evidence from whatever source is relevant and identify patterns and order and use inductive reasoning to suggest what the causes are' are more suited to qualitative methods (Newby 2010: p. 46).

Qualitative research is not a singular method. In fact, methodologies within qualitative research can be so different in epistemology and practice that they sit quite uncomfortably under their shared umbrella. This puts pressure on the qualitative researcher to identify specific qualitative methods that respond to the research question(s) at hand. This is a critical phase in the development of a research project and one that Howe and Eisenhart suggest presents both opportunities and challenges. They argue that 'research questions should derive data collection techniques and analysis rather than vice versa' (Howe and Eisenhart 1990: p. 6). While we agree, and will discuss this further later in the chapter, some qualitative researchers (e.g. Beattie 1995: p. 40) caution that there is no way to stop the research method from having an impact on the research question. They are inseparable and the research findings will be inextricably intertwined with the method.

The identification of methods appropriate to the research is made less onerous by the inherent flexibility of qualitative methodology. Denzin and Lincoln call the qualitative researcher a *Bricoleur*, or one who produces a *bricolage*, that is, a pieced-together, close-knit set of practices that provide solutions to a problem in a concrete situation (Denzin and Lincoln 1994: p. 2). As the *Bricoleur* analogy suggests, qualitative methodology is 'multi method in focus' (Denzin and Lincoln 1994: p. 2). This is not to say that qualitative methods cannot stand alone as appropriate methodologies. Indeed some, such as conversation analysis (Schegloff 2007), are sometimes only possible as single methods because their philosophy does not allow for multiple epistemological perspectives to be recruited simultaneously.

Often partnership researchers require a methodology that allows for the complexity and idiosyncrasies of diverse and complex data. Grady (1996) argues that to deal with the complexity of human experience, research should be undertaken from an informed position, which allows the researcher to 'choose challenging rhetorical and methodological tools that allow us to focus on the complexities of the practice of theory in practice' (Grady 1996: p. 70). The recruitment of qualitative methods in education research requires researchers to acknowledge the influence of their prior knowledge, attitudes and understanding of the environment or issue. Qualitative research draws on the researcher's own imagination and insights to develop perspectives and reach understandings (Newby 2010).

Mixed methods and grass-roots approaches

Teacher-research

The approaches we discuss in the remainder of this chapter have two key things in common – they are grass-roots approaches, in that they emerge from the issues and realities of a particular research site; and they orient to the importance of the teacher as a researcher. The term teacher-research 'covers a range of activities that share the idea that teachers' research questions come not only from either theoretical or practical concerns but also from the intersection of these two traditionally distinct domains' (Freebody 2003: p. 86).

As we discussed in Chapter 2, schools are complex research sites and they operate within larger, even more complex systems (Senge 2000). In many ways it is the teacher who is the critical interface between those systems and the students' educational experiences. As a result of this, over the last few decades, educators, educational authorities and policymakers have become increasingly convinced of the importance of the teacher's role in educational research, recognizing that standards of teaching and learning are unlikely to be improved through the introduction of policies that do not relate directly to the classroom as a work site for teachers and learners (Hargreaves 1999). From this recognition emerged the idea of 'the teacher-researcher'. This way of viewing teachers has multiple aims and achievements:

- It builds a more cohesive relationship between research, public policy and professional practice (Freebody, P., Freebody, K. and Maney 2011b).

- It protects teachers' professional autonomy and gives them an active role in the production of knowledge in education (Kincheloe 2003).

- It acts as a form of resistance, allowing teachers to be active in the forming of public opinion around education and giving voice to the policy silences that exist (Donald et al. 1995: p. 272).

The teacher-researcher model resulted in (and contributed to) a shift in the ways teachers were viewed, away from the idea of teacher as a transmitter of already approved knowledge, towards the idea of teacher as 'knower and thinker ... who did not need more "findings" from university-based researchers, but more dialogue with other teachers that would generate theories grounded in practice' (Cochran-Smith and Lytle 1999: p. 15). The 'teacher as knower/thinker' is central to our conception of partnership research in education. There is a plethora of research that suggests that the teacher-researcher model has many benefits including:

- opportunities for teachers to critically trial research-based suggestions in the context of their own practice (McIntyre 2005);

- the development of 'knowledge-creating schools' designed to incorporate the complementary strengths of researchers and practitioners (McIntyre 2005);

- opportunities for teachers to examine and articulate aspects of their practice (Bonne et al. 2007); and

- the development of a perception of research as relevant to classroom practice (Bonne et al. 2007).

The teacher-researcher model in partnership research, however, is not without its challenges. Forms of grass-roots research described below have been described as 'cheap on money but dear on time' (Donald et al. 1995: p. 27). Involving partners in research often requires them to extend the definition of their role, which can mean additional work and more pressure for those involved. As much as this may improve aspects of teaching or learning, directly or otherwise, for the participants, it often and unfortunately ends with little recognition for this extra work. In our experience, partnership research with teachers is most successful when it engages a whole school or community in the inquiry. This leads to work that is both relevant to the participants, valued by the leadership, and as a result, more likely to be sustainable beyond the project itself.

Action research

Action research is a methodological process that has emerged from the teacher-researcher model. Rather than a methodology, action research is considered an 'orientation to inquiry with an obligation to action' (Groundswater-Smith and Irwin 2011). Sometimes known as participatory action research, practitioner research, or action learning, action research involves practitioners (such as teachers) taking on the dual roles of practitioners and researchers to explore a problem or issue within their own professional practice. Through this, practitioners develop a better understanding of a phenomenon by actively changing the ways that that phenomenon is practiced/manifested within the site of inquiry. Action research is firmly grounded in the local. It is a transformational process that uses systematic forms of inquiry (methods) to provide participants with insight into a question or issue that is relevant to them and the site they work in (Groundswater-Smith and Irwin 2011). In educational settings, action research usually involves teachers examining their practice, often with the help of university academics or education department officers (Kemmis and McTaggart 2005). As a result, the line between research and practice can often blur when teachers are engaged in action research (Borko, Whitcomb and Byrnes 2008).

Despite differences in design, all action research incorporates two features – intentionality and systematicity (Cochran-Smith and Donnell 2006). Action research is intentional. It is a deliberate activity that requires planning and design – it is not ad hoc or spontaneous. The systematicity refers to the organized nature of the data collection. In other words, action research is a research project that engages the practitioner as both participant and researcher, it involves a planned investigation or intervention with organized data collection that is specific and appropriate to both the research goal (or research questions) and the research site. The grass-roots, site-specific nature of action research acts as both an advantage and a challenge. As already discussed, practitioner research allows for a focus on issues that are of immediate concern to those in the industry. It also allows for a growth in research expertise and research culture in schools. It can, however, be challenging to make the research significant past the immediate impact on site. To make the findings relevant and accessible to others – to make the knowledge matter – researchers need to be aware of how the research will be presented and reported outside of the research site. Two key concepts that are central to this are collaboration and rigour. While they may seem an odd combination, they are necessary and both need to be considered in the early planning of the research. Collaboration in action research can be achieved through various research partners, critical friends, academic mentors, or by organizing data collection across various sites or disciplines. While it may be the case that 'too many cooks' could confuse the work, it is also the case that the more people involved, and the more people with different roles in the work (principals, regional officers, teachers, academics, etc.), the more perspectives are available and the more likelihood of institutional impact (Borko, Whitcomb and Byrnes 2008). If, coupled with this collaboration, the research is considered rigorous, then a community of researchers and practitioners are able use the research to inform their own work in different sites. While action research is also specific to the site it takes place in, it often maintains its rigour through planning and reporting the research in conventional ways – stating clear research questions, outlining methodologies and data collection, and analysing using developed methodologies.

The methods used within action research projects are often those associated with qualitative research more generally. Regardless of the particulars of the research project, action research tends to follow a structure that includes planning, implementing, reflecting, revising and reporting as detailed in Figure 8.1.

The cycles displayed in Figure 8.1 are self-reflective, in that in order to be successful the participants/researchers need to reflect on their practice before, during and after the 'action' or intervention takes place. Acknowledging once again that all action research projects differ depending on local circumstances, the general sequence of a project involves:

- Identifying an area of practice that would benefit from investigation.
- Planning a change.
- Acting on the plan and observing the process.
- Reflecting on the action, this may include exploring data collected during the process.
- Re-planning one's practice in order to accommodate the findings.
- Further action on the new plan, more reflection, and so on.

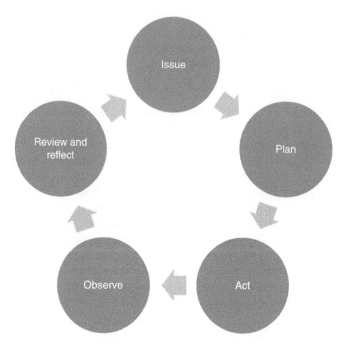

Figure 8.1 *The Action Research Cycle, modified from Newby 2010*

As Kemmis and McTaggart (2005) point out, the actual process of action research may not be as neat as this cycle suggests, phases can often overlap and, because much action research is collaborative, may vary from participant to participant. This variability, along with the negotiated nature of the process, means that action research lacks the formality of other approaches (Newby 2010). This is neither positive nor negative, but influences the use of action research beyond the participants involved – in other words effects the particular ways in which we can make knowledge matter. Many advocates of action research see it as one of the most influential research processes in education because it is rooted in classroom practice and the everyday realities of working in a school. Others, however, have expressed concern about the rigour and trustworthiness of the results, and the ability for the research to have an effect beyond the single classroom (Newby 2010). For researchers aiming to produce findings that are both locally contextualized and generalizable for a wider system, design-based research procedures have incorporated elements of practitioner research with a deeper focus on research rigour.

Design-based research

A relatively new research method, Design-based research (DBR) was developed specifically for use in educational settings. DBR is informed by both action research practices and experimental laboratory research. Like action research, it is a grass-roots approach; with the research focus specific to the particular site in which the research is taking place. However, like laboratory research, DBR follows a structure of design, collection and analysis that incorporates theory building and testing. Essentially, DBR can be 'characterised as an inter-disciplinary mixed method approach conducted "in the field" that serves applied and theory-building purposes' (Reimann 2011: p. 37). It was developed by Brown (1992) and Collins (1992) to make education research more relevant for teaching practices by linking theory and practice more strongly to educational research (Reimann 2011). This linking is achieved in DBR through the development of research projects with local relevance and the implementation of research in authentic settings. Wang and Hannafin (2005) characterize DBRs as:

- Pragmatic – usually intervention-orientated and designed to take place in real world settings.

- Grounded in theory and research – unlike other forms of practitioner research, DBRs must evolve from an interpretive framework and/or instructional theory.

- Flexible, iterative and interactive – the research should be modified based reflection from participants and findings from data collection.

- Integrative – the research needs to fit in with, and be part of, the school community.

- Contextual – the elements of the research (interpretive framework, methodology, design) need to be appropriately aligned and the research as a whole needs to work within the wider context of the school and system.

Often a DBR focuses on a single issue that has both local relevance to the research site, as well as broader relevance to the educational research and practice more generally. Therefore, DBRs can be roughly characterized as projects that are informed by broader educational theory, but emerging from local issues. DBRs in the field of education are generally teacher-led, with teacher learning central to the design (Bannan-Ritland 2008), with a community of educational leaders and researches brought in as needed for support. Often academic researchers act as 'critical friends' and offer help planning, documenting and disseminating the research. DBR is also an effective method for studies that wish to understand a phenomenon or test the effectiveness of a theory in multiple sites. For example, a research team may wish to understand how a particular framework can be applied in literacy teaching. Teachers in multiple sites may be given the framework and asked to plan an intervention, using the framework, for their classroom. The research team would support the teachers, providing them with guidance on intervention design, data collection and analysis. Each site would then produce a report of their intervention. Collectively, these reports would form the data for the wider study.

Unlike other research methodologies (experiments, discourse analysis, case studies, etc.), DBRs do not have a specific method; rather they follow a framework or philosophy of ongoing data-collection (Reimann 2011) and therefore each project is unique. Having said this, the DBR process generally consists of four elements:

1 informed planning and implementation of a project;

2 continual trialling and taking stock where the project is modified or redesigned according to ongoing data collection;

3 evaluation of local impact upon completion of the project; and

4 evaluation of the potential for broader impact in the education field more generally.

Like action research, DBR takes place in cycles, with a focus on testing and revising the study as necessary during the process (rather than at the end). Incorporating the four elements listed above, and acknowledging that all DBRs are different, Reimann (2011: p. 40) suggests three main phases and typical activities of a DBR process. They are:

Phase 1 – Preparing the experiment:

- Clarifying goals

- Documenting starting points

- Outlining an envisioned learning trajectory.

Phase 2 – Experimenting to support learning:

- Collecting data in cycles of design and analysis (as discussed above and similar to the action research process)

- Applying interpretive frameworks

- Formulating and testing domain-specific theories.

Phase 3 – Conducting retrospective analyses:

- Outlining the rationale for the interpretive framework and methods in light of the data and results

- Establishing trust in the findings (ensuring and highlighting the rigour of the study)

- Ensuring repeatability
- Ensuring generalizability.

It is in this last phase that a major distinction between action research (and other forms of practitioner research) and DBR are evident. Although DBR is conceived as grass-roots, as a method it is concerned with making a difference to wider systems – local studies that have global impact. A major phase in the work is ensuring the results of the local 'test' can be replicated and distributed. Therefore, it is key that the study is explicit, trustworthy, generalizable and repeatable.

It is common for DBRs to continue for an extended duration, weeks or months, and rather than having one fixed data collection point, evaluation is continual over that time. This extended time frame is necessary for the research to capture the success or otherwise of the intervention. Owing to the nature of work in schools, change can be a slow process and therefore any intervention study must allow enough time for change to take hold. This means that, while DBR is a method designed specifically for research in education settings, it is only appropriate for studies that seek to either test or understand a facet of educational theory, and then, only if there is enough time allocated to the study. DBR also relies heavily on in-school research participants who are able (and willing) to take on the role of 'lead researcher' in their site – in charge of design, collection and reporting of data. The teacher-led aspect of DBR is essential for achieving long-term research. It is also the case that external researchers may only visit a site a discrete number of times; but to have teachers, who are always on-site, as key members of the research team allows for continuous testing and improvement. Finally, an important benefit of DBR is its ability to develop capacity in teachers and schools not only to implement, but to *generate* sustainable innovations.

Applied theatre as research

Theatre techniques can be effectively integrated throughout research processes. It is also recognized that forms of theatre-making can be a complete research methodology, rather than just a tool utilized within another approach (Lea et al. 2011; Gallagher 2011; Norris 2009). As ways of learning, there are many commonalities between drama and qualitative research (Henry 2000). Both require:

- a sensitive and self-reflexive response to the environment;
- a willingness to improvise and to take risks;
- the employment of multiple roles and changing settings; and
- a willingness to engage with narrative.

Furthermore, both engage with:

- tacit knowledge involving affect and intuition;

- personal and social realities;

- metaphors and symbols to communicate meanings; and

- ways of knowing which people use in their everyday lives. (Henry 2000: p. 51)

In much applied theatre, topics, themes or problems are explored through drama with a group of people. Participants can take on many roles: planning, acting in role, reflecting and critiquing out of role, and presenting their work. Applied theatre might involve the participants working directly with an experience or issue from their own lives, or they might work analogously through a fictional frame; either way, the theatre forms used are designed to create a safe and critical distance from a subject (Fels 2011; Fels and Belliveau 2008; Gallagher 2011). A variety of theatrical traditions might be used: researching, writing and performing a scripted play (Norris 2009); verbatim theatre and storytelling (Anderson and Wilkinson 2007), participatory improvisation (Fels 2011; Gallagher 2011); contemporary performance-art (Hughes et al. 2011); forum theatre (Boal 1979), process drama (Heathcote 1984), or site specific performance (Hughes et al. 2011; Ledgard 2007; MacNamara and Rooke 2007). Applied theatre can engage people in identifying problems, considering diverse issues, experience and perspectives, and imagining/enacting possible solutions or futures.

Both Cahill (2006) and Conrad (2004), argue that there are many similarities between action research and applied theatre. Applied theatre, like action research, often involves a process of inquiry, based on a topic, theme or problem relevant to the participants (Nicholson 2005; Prendergast and Saxton 2009; Prentki and Preston 2009; Thompson 2006). Cahill observes that both traditions 'are centrally concerned with dialogue, praxis, participatory exploration and transformation' and involve 'collective processes of enquiry, action and reflection (Cahill 2006: p. 62). In both processes the relationship between the researcher/practitioner and participants is a collaborative one. Applied theatre, then, like action research, has the potential to be an affective methodology for research with young people. As Wyn and White argue (1997) young people tend to be excluded from problem-solving activities relating to their own affairs and are commonly pathologized or glamorized in health and education discourses and, once relegated to the role of object of research, can only with difficulty be seen as the source of solutions (Cahill 2006: p. 63).

What drama and Applied Theatre as Research achieves, which most other research methods do not, are emotional and aesthetic, multi-modal (aural, oral, kinaesthetic and symbolic) forms of interaction and representation

(Cahill 2006: p. 63). Reflecting on her experience of using drama to research with urban high school students, Gallagher comments: 'Led by art, researchers, teacher, and students moved differently: We created an experiment in research that changed the terms of engagement' (Gallagher 2007; 2011: p. 328). She found that researching through drama made possible different modes of communication, conduct and embodiment (Gallagher 2008). She also argued that drama gives participants as co-researchers the opportunity for '*self*-representation', whereas in other methodologies it is the researcher who represents the research participants:

> This is theatre as methodology, theatre as a mode of devising a meta-world; to collaboratively and artistically frame a 'real' research problem or context in order to peer inside it. Engaging youth in research – theatrically – provides a robust environment for questioning, as the work deals in metaphor, or recreates 'real life' situations in which collaborators are able to more freely experiment with alternative strategies and perspectives in testing the validity of their own theories and insights about the world. (Gallagher 2011: p. 328)

The following case study provides an example of arts-informed methodologies in health research. While we realize that this study does not concern itself with education, we have included it because it provides not only an illustration of emerging methodologies, but also demonstrates innovative approaches to research dissemination, which will be explored further in Chapter 10.

Case Study 6

Case study name: Designing, Implementing and Assessing Arts-Based Methods of Knowledge Translation in Research Ethics.

Grant funder: University of British Columbia Humanities and Social Science (HSS) Research Fund/College for Interdisciplinary Studies HSS Research Grants.

Research team: George Belliveau, Theatre Education; Susan M. Cox and Darquise Lafrenière, Centre for Applied Ethics; Donal O'Donoghue, Visual Art Education; and Rena Sharon, School of Music (University of British Columbia).

Partners: More than 50 artists and researchers.

Research team for larger study: Susan M. Cox, Principal Investigator; Michael McDonald, Co-Principal Investigator; Patricia Kaufert, Joseph Kaufert, and Anne Townsend, Co-Investigators.

Case Study 6

Location: British Columbia, Canada. The larger study was located in Canada at the University of British Columbia (UBC) and the University of Manitoba.

Brief project description: This eighteen-month project explored the opportunity and potential for arts-based approaches in the dissemination of results from a larger, five-year long, study exploring participation in health research (see the discussion for more information on this). The project involved an interdisciplinary group of scholars from the arts (particularly theatre, music and visual art) and ethics. These scholars worked with professional artists to create, perform, or display artworks written using research data to communicate research findings. The artforms recruited for this study included 'found' poetry, whereby 'the researcher uses only the words of the participant(s) to create a poetic rendition of a story or phenomenon' (Butler-Kisber 2002: p. 232), visual arts, song, and drama. These artefacts were combined in a performance which disseminated the research findings to its audience – 'to give voice to the experiences of human subjects [sic] enrolled in many types of health research, e.g. clinical trials, behavioural, biomedical or public health studies, and generate greater understanding of and respect for human subjects amongst various audiences' (Lafreniere et al. 2013, p. 245).

Because this research project was nested in a larger study, this project examined questions of dissemination informed by the research questions of the larger study and as an example of arts-informed inquiry (e.g. Knowles and Cole 2008), the description of the study provided here is unable to capture its complexity. In many ways, this project employed methods recognizable in case-study research more generally; interviews with participants were collected and coded according to the themes of participation, practical costs, relationships and trust. The researchers working in the four different art forms used the same interviews, but adapted the methodological approaches depending on the demands of the dissemination through the art form. Feedback was sought from those that created the art forms (the artists and researchers) on the process of the research and from the audience on their understanding of the research and their response to the art.

Discussion: This case is remarkable for several reasons. Firstly, it is a research project that worked in partnership with another research project. This pilot study was actually a project undertaken as part of the dissemination strategy of a much larger, five-year study. The larger study was titled *Centring the Human Subject in Health Research: Understanding the Meaning and Experience of Research Participation* and was funded by the Canadian Institute for Health Research. This study sees two different research teams working in partnership with one another exploring similar issues.

Case Study 6

This research also sought to address a perceived gap in the field of arts-based research, that 'while different methodological perspectives on engaging the arts in research have been advanced, questions of ethics have, in large part, been neglected. Consequently methodological and theoretical frameworks for other researchers and artists interested in this breakthrough work are lacking' (Boydell et al. 2012). Therefore, in addition to their need to meet the needs of the research partners and the partner research project, this study has informed several academic papers specifically exploring methodological questions regarding ethics, authorship and 'truth' in research (see Lafreniere et al. 2013).

Further information: The results of this study took the form of displayed poetry and visual art, and performed theatre and music. The performance piece was performed twice for two different audiences: participants in the research, and members of the wider community, including interested academics. As well as these two live performances, a video of the performance has been created and shown at a variety of events for different audiences. As well as the artefacts from the research, this research has been used to inform workshops for those interested in working with arts-based methodologies (see Boydell et al. 2012), and has been the basis of journal articles (see Lafreniere et al. 2013).

Conclusion

As we argued at the beginning of this chapter, attention to methodology is at the heart of successful research. Partnership research in education can take many forms and different projects will have different methodological requirements. This chapter has provided a brief outline of quantitative and qualitative research philosophies, with the acknowledgement that each of the epistemological research stances are worthy of their own book. We have also used this chapter to explore some particular methodologies that have significance for partnership research in education. Action research, design-based research, and applied theatre as research are all grass-roots methods that have been developed to meet perceived needs in education research – whether it is new ways of finding and displaying research data, new ways of involving research participants, attention to how practitioners can research their own practice, or new ways of providing frameworks for schools to develop context-specific projects within a broader research question – each of these methodologies offer partnership researchers with new ways of engaging research participants and audiences.

Key messages from the chapter

- Methods and methodologies are at the heart of any research, and deciding which methods best suit which research is key to a successful research project.

- Research in education serves particular purposes and audiences, and to make knowledge matter in education, research must attend to the complex relationship between teaching practice, school leadership and public policy, and find methods to explore that relationship.

- Quantitative research methods emerge from the philosophical principle of positivism. This guiding principle is the belief that truth can only be discovered through verifiable facts – that we only know what we can prove through data.

- Grass-roots approaches emerge from the issues and realities of a particular research site; and they orient to the importance of the teacher as a researcher.

- The 'teacher as knower/thinker' is central to our conception of partnership research in education. There is a plethora of research that suggests that the teacher-researcher model has many benefits including: opportunities for critical reflection, the development of knowledge generated in schools, an examination of practice and a growing understanding of the relevance of research to classroom practice.

- Action research is a methodological process that has emerged from the teacher-researcher model. Rather than a methodology, action research is considered an 'orientation to inquiry with an obligation to action' (Groundswater-Smith and Irwin 2011).

CHAPTER NINE

Developing doctoral research partnerships

Much of the book so far has focused on you (the reader) being a or the primary investigator in the research being undertaken. In this chapter we want to spend some time discussing other, equally important ways that we are involved in partnership research in education. To borrow and adapt a piece of communal knowledge – it takes a village to do education well. Those that work in education know the necessity of so many different roles – teachers, students, parents, principals, regional officers, home-school liaison officers, teacher-trainers, educational researchers, politicians, the list goes on. The relationship between all of these 'villagers' can be difficult to navigate at times. While all of these roles have different tasks, purposes and relationships to each other, they are also dependent on each other and, when done effectively are usually highly collaborative. Beyond official partnerships, educational researchers are often asked to act as a 'critical friend' for the development of programmes, teacher research, and other academic research, including research higher degrees (RHD) be they honours, masters or PhD students. It is also the case that for many academics the most common form of partnership research they engage in is with their RHD students. While acknowledging overlap, this chapter is separated in two distinct sections. Firstly, we explore the role of the 'critical friend' in education research. Looking at how research may benefit from your input as a critical outsider and exploring what this looks like at different phases of a research project. Secondly, this chapter explores the characteristics of productive partnerships with RHD students. Here we consider ethical and organizational issues in the students-supervisor relationship as well as guidelines for the successful doctoral research.

Being a critical friend

Earlier in this book we discussed the multiple layers within education that research needs to be significant to make knowledge matter. This, coupled with the fact that research is a 'messy matter' (Newby 2010: p. 28) means that having critical friends, people inside the profession but outside the research, can allow researchers to conduct their project in a more purposeful, targeted and rigorous way. Good critical friends, the collective noun for which may be an 'advisory board', can not only give feedback on the different processes of the project, but can give advice and assistance in practical matters such as obtaining research sites and disseminating the findings of the work in different corners of the education system. This section, therefore, is about both why and how critical friends can be employed in partnership research and what we believe are key duties associated with being an effective critical friend. In other chapters we have discussed the ways researchers can use critical friends in their projects. In this chapter we would like to shift the focus to being an effective critical friend – which we feel is a key role for researchers and supervisors. Much of our discussion here focuses on the critical friend who is an academic, giving advice and guidance around research processes, as this is often the case in educational research. Having said this, it is also common to have an advisory board that includes government or departmental employees who have insight into the development of policy and professional programmes.

Being a critical friend is not a 'one size fits all' task. Different research studies require different levels of input at different stages. Before we explore these differences more thoroughly, let's examine some general principles:

- When you accept an invitation to be a critical friend, be clear about what you can offer the project. This refers to both your expertise – for example you may be well versed in the chosen methodology but not know very much about the issue being researched – and the pragmatics – such as how much time you have to give or your availability during the research period. Do not accept an invitation if you do not think you can contribute to the project. It is better for the research team to spend an extra week finding another critical friend at the beginning, than a year chasing you for feedback.

- Be critical. It sounds obvious but can actually be difficult, particularly if you are giving a response to the work of a colleague or someone who is more senior in their area. There are sensitive and tactful ways of giving useful, critical feedback. As tempting as it may be, being 'pleasant' is not useful to the research partners and can result in everyone (including you) doing their role badly. It's better to hear the truth from a critical friend than survey the smoking ruin of a research project.

- Give feedback in a variety of ways. Responding to documents and drafts is vital, but it is also helpful to provide additional readings that support your feedback. This allows the research team to understand your perspective more comprehensively and to develop a more rounded idea of what you are attempting to communicate. Also be willing to discuss your feedback if there are questions arising from this process.

- Keep your feedback user-friendly. Remember that you have been asked for input because you are an 'expert' in the area that others in the research team may not know much about. It is easy to forget that our expertise has been developed over a long period of time and through a variety of sources. If we forget this there is a danger that our feedback can be inaccessible to the people we are trying to support. It is worth talking to the partners about their level of familiarity with research terminology. This varies greatly from partner to partner.

As we have already discussed, different research requires different inputs. As much as all research is different, however, there are three main research phases in which feedback from critical friends is commonly sought: planning, implementation, and dissemination.

Planning

Critical friends are recruited during planning phases of research, both formally and informally. Formal critical friends are often associated with giving feedback to RHD students under circumstances such as PhD confirmation processes or as readers for grant applications. In fact, if you work in academia giving this kind of formal feedback is commonplace. Many academics would have general guidelines issues, or features they look for during this process. These include:

- Whether the research question aligns with the data gathering and analysis plan – in other words, is the researcher able to answer the proposed questions using the proposed data? This may seem obvious but quite often the research questions are seeking to understand a phenomenon that is not actually evident in the data. A common example of this is a study that seeks to explore how something happens in the classroom and only plans to conduct interviews. Interviews tell us a participant's perception of events, not the actuality of the events themselves. To understand a phenomenon a researcher or research team must observe it – either in person or through recordings.

- Whether the research is making assumptions about what is already known. Asking how a phenomenon works assumes that the phenomenon exists. For example, asking 'how do teachers use the quality teaching frameworks in their planning?' assumes that teachers do, in fact, use quality teaching frameworks. If such questions are being asked, the study must establish how this assumption is known (usually through previous research).

- Whether the project has situated itself within a wider body of educational theory/research.

- Whether the project has established the significance of the inquiry and the 'research gap' that needs to be filled. These elements of the research planning (and the elements above) usually require a review of current literature and research. A critical reader will be looking for the research to fill a specific need – this establishes its significance within the wider body of knowledge.

- Whether the timeline is appropriate. This seems obvious but, in our experience, remains one of the most common issues in research planning. The general rule is that research always takes longer than you imagine. As we have mentioned in other chapters, schools are busy places – establishing a relationship and building trust takes time. The busyness of schools and the realities of researchers leading busy multifaceted lives means that timelines routinely lengthen if not blow out all together.

When being an informal critical friend, it is more likely that you will be asked to respond to a more finite element of the research planning and the process is therefore much more ad hoc. We suggest, for those that are new to the experience of providing critical feedback on others' research, that you use the above guidelines (and any others that are relevant to your work) to establish a pro forma you can use when reading research proposals. This is also a useful resource to give your own RHD students or teacher research participants.

Implementation

There are many ways you can be involved in the implementation of a project as a critical friend. Often, particularly when grass-roots methods such as design-based research or action research are employed, academics are called upon by school practitioners to provide support for the research. In these cases, teachers may collect and organize data and then work with academics to undertake the analysis and determine the results. When working as a critical friend during the implementation of a project, it is worthwhile establishing what skills the research team already possess and finding out what you can offer. Many teachers have a general understanding of educational research but do not have formal training and little experience in research methodologies. Therefore, they can identify a problem for investigation and organize data collection but often find the next steps challenging not because they are not capable, but because they are not sure of the procedures of analysis and are not sufficiently experienced in the processes of educational research. Conversely, sometimes educators and educational researchers are called on as critical friends by researchers from other fields to provide guidance about the protocols of working in educational research sites. Schools run to their own agendas and to their own timetables. There are particular 'ways of knowing and doing' in schools that make engaging in research challenging for those unaccustomed to the pace and complexity of school environments. There are also specific ethical issues associated with conducting research with children that researchers from other fields may not have experienced. Educational researchers provide an 'insiders view' of the research site that can assist researchers from other areas to navigate the idiosyncrasies of various education research sites.

Dissemination

Being a critical friend during the dissemination phase of a research project usually requires a significant amount of reading. Most feedback during the dissemination phase is given about whether the report (PhD, article or other form of dissemination) is structured and written clearly and communicates effectively. Critical friends are best able to give advice if they have had minimal prior contact with the research and so can make a judgement about whether all the relevant information is available and the results are presented in a way that is appropriate, rigorous and clearly structured. Another way that critical friends can be useful during dissemination is to provide advice about how the project could be disseminated. Beyond the usual required report, dissemination should target audiences in both schools and in the academy. Critical friends in the dissemination stage can provide research partners with an understanding of how research results can be communicated to different audiences. Critical friends often have highly developed understandings of the kinds of audiences different journals have or publishers who have an interest in their field. This is a kind of social capital that experienced researchers build up over their career and is rarely written down. Rather, this kind of understanding is passed on through discussions at conferences or in the context of a critical friendship discussion. These professional conversations are highly valuable as they assist researchers to target their work to the right audiences. If critical friends are able to, it is also appropriate for them to connect researchers to their networks to assist the researcher or research team to communicate the outcomes of their research to the widest possible audience.

  If you have been a critical friend you will find many of those skills are readily applicable to the role of being a research higher-degree supervisor.

Being a supervisor

Having the opportunity to do a research thesis – to devote time and energy exploring a particular aspect of education that interests you regardless of whether it interests others or brings in research funding is a real privilege. It may not feel like a privilege when a student is in the middle of the work, but there are precious few times in our professional lives that we are presented with the opportunity to do research work simply because we want to. Most often, we do work that is fundable, or work that directly relates to current policy to establish concrete results or change in the profession. Research theses are one of the few times,[1] in the current funding-driven climate of the academy, where we have the opportunity to explore theories and practices of education out of our own curiosity. Not only is it a privilege, it is also vital for the continued development of our field to be conducting work not just beyond, but often in spite of, current practices and ideologies.

You might think that being an 'expert' in education would mean that those working in educational research and academia would be good RHD supervisors – that they would understand how to facilitate the work of others, provide guidance, establish a rapport, and communicate clear and high expectations. Talking to RHD students, however, we find that this is not always the case. Many students find doing a research degree in education an extremely isolating and frustrating experience. There are a variety of possible reasons for this dissatisfaction. Unlike other fields, education does not often have a cohort of research students working on a large project (as can be found in science or medicine). It is also the case that RHDs in education are often also professionals working as teachers or school leaders and do not have the time and energy to become immersed in academic life the way students in other fields can. The fact that so many of our students are part-time in their studies while they work full-time in an education setting may have allowed some institutions to skimp on the support available for these students. Research students are central to our field – they are the future of educational research, not only in terms of what research is undertaken, but will also be the future research leaders supervising research in education. This makes the partnership between research student and supervisor one of the most critical research partnerships in education. It is imperative that research students are given access to research training in a variety of research methods, not just the methods involved in their own study. It is also vital that RHD students in education have positive and productive partnerships with both their supervisors and their research partners/participants. These experiences lay the foundations for the kinds of

---

[1]We are aware that RHD students are often tied to projects not of their own choosing out of policy or because they are on scholarship. In our experience, however, in research careers this opportunity to explore an interest that springs from curiosity is a normal part of a career in educational research.

research they will undertake in the future. This section explores some of the logistics of the research supervision process, including ethics, guidelines for supervisors and students, and suggestions for the dissemination of RHD student's research outcomes.

Responsibility and ownership

There is obviously something 'inherent' in the supervisor–student partnership because, when you think about it, there are some complex elements that, for the most part, appear to be unproblematic in most supervisor–student relationships. Perhaps it is because the mentoring/apprenticeship model is so enduring that we take these issues for granted. When we do struggle, however, the complexity of the relationship can mean that things do not just go a little wrong. We will discuss what to do when things go wrong later in this chapter, but we would like to focus here on the complex questions around ownership and responsibility in RHD research.

As we discussed earlier, embarking on your own research project is a wonderful (stressful, exciting, frustrating) privilege. For this reason, we encourage the students we supervise to consider developing and implementing their own research project for their RHD. This, of course, is not always the case and is not always possible. Some students receive scholarships or entry into RHD programmes on the condition they work within a larger, already developed, project. In these cases, the issue of 'ownership' is clearer. When the project is designed by the research student (we hope, in consultation with their supervisor), then the research belongs to the student and supervisors and critical friends should respect this arrangement. That said, it is the role of the supervisor to ensure the research is achievable in scale and in scope. Supervisors have a duty of care to ensure the student is given the best opportunities to achieve and succeed in the degree. If a student designs a study that is impractical or methodologically misaligned, it is the supervisor's responsibility to ensure it is modified to make the research project viable and successful. This point segues into questions about who is responsible for the research. Essentially, the responsibility of the research is shared. On one level, the student is responsible for planning, implementing and disseminating the research. It is, after all, their project and their learning process. For administration purposes, however, the supervisor is usually the chief investigator of the research. This means that, according to the institution, the responsibility of the research falls to the supervisor. This is potentially problematic – as chief investigator, the supervisor must ensure all ethical procedures are followed (including in many cases being responsible for the storage of data). Finding the balance between ownership and responsibility of the research is something that we recommend supervisors and students explicitly communicate about, perhaps even using a template or contract to define and record how each role will contribute to high quality research.

Ethics

We have discussed the ethical issues sometimes involved in partnership in education research in Chapter 7. We mention it again here, however, because ethical considerations for doctoral theses have additional elements and complexities beyond those outside a structured RHD programme. When working as a supervisor of a doctoral thesis you have two, hopefully not competing, duties of care – one is to your RHD student and the other to the participants in their research study. As the supervisor, you are responsible for the effect that participation in the study has on the research 'subjects' and partners. It is your role to ensure that the data collection process causes no harm. For many educators this may sound like an obvious statement – cause no harm is a central tenet of working with children. As a researcher, however, this has practical implications that may not be expected. It calls into question the ethics of, for example, using control groups and allowing some students access to a programme and denying other students. While not insurmountable, these implications should be addressed in the research planning.

It is also your role as a supervisor to care for your student. To ensure that they are not exploited, that they are well placed to be awarded their degree, and are not put in a situation where their lack of knowledge could have an adverse effect. In other words, your student needs to be allowed to learn how to be a researcher in a safe space. Work with young people can be 'high stakes' ethically. Your RHD student should not be put in a situation where their inexperience as a researcher affects either their ability to do the work or their ability to do the work safely and ethically. This requires you to be involved in the practical research work of your student. By this we do not mean that you must accompany them for their data collection or liaise with participants, but that you should know what, when and how your student is planning to carry out their research. If university or organizational ethical clearance is required, this should be sought under your guidance.

Managing the supervisor–co-supervisor–student triangle

Choosing a co-, associate or secondary supervisor is a key part of producing productive RHD work. Secondary supervisors can be chosen for a variety of reasons. We suggest that the supervisor and student have a frank conversation where they informally (or formally, if you'd prefer) 'audit' what they can offer each other and the process. A secondary supervisor can then be selected who can assume a particular role or add a particular skill. Some common, and often successful, reasons for choosing a secondary supervisor include their particular methodological expertise, their experience in the profession, or their understanding of the theory that the research is grounded in. Other, more general considerations for choosing a secondary supervisor include:

- Time allocation – many primary supervisors are extremely busy and so a secondary supervisor who has more time to read drafts and give feedback can become important.

- General research project expertise – if the primary supervisor is expert in the theoretical and methodological needs of the project then a secondary supervisor who is knowledgeable in the logistics of RHD processes and thesis writing could be desirable.

- Connections or contacts – for research undertaken in a field such as education, a secondary supervisor with strong networks can be very valuable.

- Research 'clout' – while we do not recommend this as a main reason for supervisor choice, those that are well regarded in the field can sometimes offer students opportunities and expertise. It must also be acknowledged that these supervisors are often busy people and therefore students should have realistic expectations regarding what assistance they will receive from supervisors with this kind of seniority and experience.

Essentially, the type of supervisory arrangement that works will depend on the student and the nature of the research project. Having said that, we would caution supervisors and students against what we believe are some common, yet not-very-good reasons for choosing a secondary supervisor. The most obvious of these being because the person is a friend of either the supervisor or the student. While both authors have worked with friends successfully, it has sometimes been in spite of the friendship, rather than because if it, and there have always been reasons outside of the friendship for us to chose to work together (such as the reasons already cited). Above and beyond the obvious issues that can arise when one works with their friend, within the 'triangle' of supervision partnerships, two friends can affect the balance of the triangle and place pressure on the third member. We also suggest that supervisors and students resist institutional pressure to take on a supervisor simply because that person has not reached their 'student allocation'. Both the supervisor and the student should have met the proposed secondary supervisor before they commit to the project and everyone needs to feel comfortable that they can work together productively. It is a long, complex, and at times stressful relationship that needs to be grounded in common interests and respect.

No matter what the reason for the choice of the secondary supervisor, explicit roles should be established. Some research partnerships are comfortable as triangles, where each supervisor gives advice, meets with the student (either together or separately), gives feedback and responds to queries in a way that appears quite fluid. Most partnerships, however, require at least some shared understanding of who is in charge of what. Here are three suggested ways the triangle could be organized:

1   *The secondary supervisor gives very specific feedback on their area of expertise.* This may be in relation to the methodology and methods of the project, or the theoretical background of the area being studied. For example, a study exploring how geography education techniques could be used to teach values in school might have a primary supervisor in the values education area. The secondary supervisor could be someone who works in geography education and could provide feedback on the traditions and approaches of geography curricula in schools, the theoretical frame works that geography aligns with, and the practical design of teaching and learning in geography.

2   *The secondary supervisor assists the student in the field.* If the secondary supervisor is one that works in the professional field that the research relates to, it might be appropriate for them to take on the role of liaison between the student and the profession more widely. This could include supporting research-site selection, introducing the student to relevant professionals at conferences or events and helping the student to navigate the data collection in the sites. For example, a study that explored the effects of community attitudes to a government housing site on the students in a local primary school might have a primary supervisor in social work or community development. The secondary supervisor could assist the RHD student to organize the logistics of data collection in the school, help the student to understand the protocols of working in schools (including interview techniques with children), and introduce the student to other educators who might be interested in their work.

3   *The secondary supervisor as a critical friend.* If the secondary supervisor has been chosen for more general reasons, they might be best placed to act as a critical friend for the study. Often, this involves being a critical reader. Both the primary supervisor and the student can be, at times, too close to the research to be able to see it from an outsider's perspective. A supervisor who understands the background and intent of the research but is still a relative 'outsider' can be beneficial during the write-up of the research.

There are other ways that supervisory team can be organized, these suggestions are merely that – suggestions. It is also the case that research projects require different roles at different stages of the research and a secondary supervisor may take on more than one or perhaps all three of these organization roles at different times in the research.

Guidelines for productive partnerships

We cannot stress enough how important explicit communication is in building productive partnerships. It is, we believe, *the key* to ensuring that supervision relationships run smoothly. Without it, expectations become fuzzy, time is wasted trying to establish what needs to happen and when, students can become anxious because they are not sure if they are on the right track, supervisors can become anxious because they are not receiving the right kind of work, and the project can suffer as a result. We acknowledge that communication can be difficult. We have seen first-hand through the multiple supervision experiences we have been involved in (as supervisor, secondary supervisor, student, critical friend or interested spectator) that relationships are disrupted and can break down when expectations are not shared. The following suggestions are a product of this experience. These strategies can form the basis of a standard set of expectations in the supervision process:

- Students email supervisors approximately one week prior to a meeting date with a clear description of what they hope to achieve at the meeting. This may include questions they need answered or drafts they would like feedback on. Supervisors should respond confirming the meeting and add anything they would like to achieve in the meeting. This way no one is surprised or unprepared.

- Consider recording meetings. This can happen digitally, although notes of meetings usually suffice. Digital voice recording allows students to listen and discuss, and then revisit as necessary. Either way, a brief summary of the meeting should be emailed to all parties after the meeting so there is a record of the ideas and actions that emerge from the supervision meetings. This may seem like a lot of work, but actually most students find that it is extremely helpful to go over the work again and focus on the main points.

- Every six months (or more frequently depending on the project), the supervisor and student should reflect on whether the current meeting schedule and plan is working. This acknowledges a crucial and often overlooked aspect of research work – that different amounts and types of support and supervision are needed at different times in the project. For example, a student may require regular face-to-face meetings at the planning stages of the project, but may only want to meet once every few months during the writing phase.

- Do some analysis together. It is important for supervisors to discuss how to analyse data with their students. In our experience, however, nothing is more useful than the process of analysing some of the data together. This models for students what research work looks like and can give them confidence as they proceed to the analysis phase of their study.

There is a plethora of research and writing that provide students and supervisors with practical guidance for doing PhD supervision well (for a good example see Silverman 2000) Being a good supervisor is a bit of a juggling act – part colleague, part teacher, part motivator, part life-coach and part research partner. The supervisor needs to be aware of their duty of care and establish a safe and supportive environment where the student can thrive. At the same time, the relationship should be scaffolded in such a way that the student has ownership of their project and, by the end of the process, is apprenticed in the research process.

When things go wrong

The RHD supervision process in many universities is what some call the 'secret garden' model- it is relatively private and takes place 'behind closed doors' (Park 2006). Although this term is often used to demonstrate the problematic nature of supervision relationships, we would like to argue that, actually, there are some positives to this approach. A good supervisory relationship is lasting and personal, often resulting in strong bonds between supervisor and student. A supervisor is a mentor and the private nature of the relationship allows each student to be treated individually. It also gives students space to work through their project and develop their ideas without too many conflicting voices or opinions. Having said that, when the relationship does not thrive, the 'secret garden model' becomes problematic, allowing for relationships to become toxic and students to flounder without support. Generally, universities have become better at establishing support systems for students and supervisors, with annual reviews and programme administrator roles. Essentially though, the supervisor and student still navigate the process alone (or almost alone). It is difficult to provide a set of guidelines for when things break down in this process because there are too many variables (the most obvious being the personalities of those involved); however, the Australian National University offers general advice for those facing problems:

- act early, before the issue establishes itself;
- act locally, start with the person immediately concerned before involving others;
- keep records; and
- seek advice.

Remember that it is a long relationship (even 'quick' PhDs usually end up taking three to four years), and should be a time in which the student is learning and discovering. It may seem easier to ignore problems in the relationship and avoid conflict – it almost never is.

Conclusion

We would like to conclude this chapter by re-stating our belief that doing research that interests us for the sake of the research idea, rather than funding or political reasons, is a great privilege. Often the one time a researcher can do this is during their PhD work and so it is imperative that research supervisors provide space, opportunity and support for novice researchers to make the most of this opportunity. This chapter has explored some of the practical aspects and issues associated with research supervision as well as exploring the role of the 'critical friend' more generally. Supporting our colleagues and students in their research endeavours is a central role as members of the academic community. It not strengthens our collegial relationships, it also provides us opportunities to be involved in and aware of new research in our field.

In the next chapter we discuss communication and dissemination strategies for partnership research. While we have placed this chapter after our discussions about data collection and data analysis we are not suggesting that research communication and dissemination should only occur after the research is concluded. In our experience, projects that communicate and disseminate during the early phases of the research build a culture of communication that augurs well for the task of publication in the post collection and post analysis phases of the research. The next chapter discusses how publication, communication and dissemination can be managed simultaneously with the other phases of partnership research.

Key messages from the chapter

- Having input from critical friends – people inside the profession but outside the research – can allow researchers to conduct their project in a more purposeful, targeted and rigorous way.

- Effective critical friends are clear about their expectations and capabilities, they are critical, they can give feedback in a variety of ways and can provide feedback that is user-friendly.

- In research that contributes to a higher degree, the responsibility of the research is shared. On one level, the student is responsible for planning, implementing and disseminating the research. It is, after all, their project and their learning process but for administration purposes the supervisor is ordinarily the chief investigator of the research.

- Partnership between research student and supervisor is one of the most critical research partnerships in education. Research students should be given access to comprehensive and diverse research training.

- The role of the supervisor is to ensure the research is achievable in scale and in scope. Supervisors have a duty of care to ensure the student is given the best opportunities to achieve and succeed in the degree. If a student designs a study that is impractical or methodologically misaligned, it is the supervisor's responsibility to ensure it is modified to make the research project is viable and successful.

CHAPTER TEN

Communicating and disseminating partnership research

Partnership researchers have a particular responsibility to share the findings from their research. In a field like education, research is taken seriously by many policymakers and practitioners when developing programmes and policy that influence learning in education settings. Partnership researchers have a responsibility to their partners but they also have a responsibility to the renewal and regeneration of theory and practice in education. A key strategy to achieve this is for researchers to develop sustainable, effective and timely approaches to communicating the outcomes of their research to the partners and the wider field. To 'make knowledge matter' in partnership research, the communication of research findings should address the multiple layers of education – from the students in the classroom, the leaders in the school, and the policymakers in the department. In this chapter we will discuss the need for effective communication and dissemination strategies through an examination of the audiences for research and the methods of reaching those audiences with timely, relevant information derived from partnership research projects. You will notice we have used two terms in this chapter; dissemination and communication. When we use the term communication we are referring to outlets for your research beyond the academic domain such as teachers, school leaders, policymakers and the community generally. In some places this is referred to as knowledge transfer. When we use the term dissemination we are referring specifically to the ways we engage with our academic colleagues to share the outcomes of our research. In our view this is not an either/or scenario. Academics have a responsibility to their colleagues but perhaps even more importantly have a responsibility to the community for whom the research serves, a community that has provided the resources for the research, to share the outcomes of the research.

Developing a communication strategy

Many researchers feel frustrated by the lack of coverage and interest that their research receives. Large and costly research projects sometimes seem to make little impact on the fields the research is carried out in. There are many reasons why this occurs. Researchers are not always skilled at developing communication strategies beyond the academy and some researchers see this as outside their job description. In our view this is short-sighted. Researchers have a responsibility that comes with research funding to provide the benefits of that research to those who have funded it. In a majority of cases those funders are governments and therefore the community through their taxes. We think a communication strategy that goes beyond academic audiences is not only desirable, but also mandatory. We intend to discuss in this chapter a range of opportunities that researchers have to share their work. Some of these opportunities relate to academic audiences but many of the communication strategies we present relate directly to the end users of our research – education systems, schools, the education leaders, teachers, parents and students.

We mentioned earlier the need to plan a dissemination and communication strategy as part of your application and planning process. We would like now to turn to the specifics of that communication and dissemination strategy and provide a discussion of approaches that are designed to reach specific audiences to increase the potential impact of your research and make the new knowledge matter. We will begin with the area that is perhaps most familiar to most researchers; dissemination to academic colleagues.

Dissemination of partnership research to academic peers

Anyone who has been active in research in the last decade will have noticed the increased emphasis being placed on publication of research. The seemingly endless quest to find a metric by which to measure researchers has led many higher education systems and many research institutions to develop measures of esteem dependent on scholarly publication of research. Simultaneously, governments who fund research have also begun developing, and in some places have fully developed, measures of research impact. Both of these measures are critical to research careers. Having said that, these two impact measures are not always aligned. For instance, if as part of your research dissemination you publish some of your findings on classroom behaviour in an introductory educational psychology textbook read by tens of thousands of students, the impact will be recognized but be of little use in many research assessment measures. There are fairly clear but not necessarily logical guidelines published by research organizations that identify acceptable outlets for published research. While this may be frustrating for some researchers, our advice is to accept and recognize that partnership research has multiple audiences that require different forms of communication. When developing a dissemination strategy consider which academic audiences will gain the most from your research and seek out the publications that those audiences read. As a general rule of thumb, the places where your academic peers search out research are likely to be the most influential in your field in terms of research reputation. The advent of search engines such as Google Scholar has allowed interdisciplinary researchers to discover research from other fields with relative ease. It is worth assessing whether your potential publication outlets can be detected through search engines of this type, to bring your research to the widest interdisciplinary audience available.

Developing protocols for academic publication

Intellectual property can be a divisive issue on partnership projects. Putting clear publication plans in place, which have been discussed and agreed upon by members of the research team and partner organization, can have the effect of avoiding these kinds of divisions. They can also support the team and enable them to write in a cohesive and comprehensive manner about the project; avoiding overlaps and ensuring the project reports on all of the relevant data. This is a kind of a mapping exercise for the publications ensuring that all of the territory is covered and that none of it is built on twice. There are two main protocols to support this process that we have used: the Project Publication Plan (PPP) and the Publication Proposal Form (PPF). The PPP is the first step in the mapping process that we have described. Put simply, it outlines the publications that will arise from the project. Table 10.1 details a PPP for a small-scale project we have recently been involved in.

The next step is to create more detail arising from this plan. In Box 10.1 we have included a Publication Proposal Form (PPF). This form arose from a large partnership research project that required a series of protocols for publication.

Table 10.1 Project publication plan (PPP) for Applied Theatre as Research Project

Publication title (working and descriptive)	Target publication	Publication type	Status
'Applied Theatre as a Research Method'	Applied Theatre Researcher	Journal article	Published
'Young Mob: A Case Study in Indigenous Performative Methods'	Performing Scholartistry	Chapter in an edited book	forthcoming
Applied Theatre and Research: Radical Departures (Title)	Applied Theatre and Research: Radical Departures	Co-authored book	Under contract

Box 10.1 Publication Proposal Form

Working title of the article:

Proposed author(s):

Publication type (please circle): A1 book, A2 other book, B1 chapter,
B2 other chapter, C1 refereed journal article, C2 other journal article, E1
refereed conference paper, E2 other conference paper or presentation, L1
major creative artwork

Anticipated length:

Brief description of content, approach and/or focus [no more than 200
words]:

Audience: [NB this is very important: – Who is this for? Why would they
need to read it? Why will they want to read it?]:

Suggested publication(s) or publisher(s) [or type, and briefly why these
are appropriate?]:

Suggested manuscript date:

Other details [no more than 150 words on any point]:

  a) what data or findings will be used & will these be readily available to
      the author/s?
  b) what assistance might be needed from others?
  c) ethical implications – eg new ethics variation required?
  d) likely photographs, illustrations, tables?
  e) other useful information?

This form was one tangible way that all of the team could be informed about
the publications in preparation. This helped to minimize overlaps and kept the
partners and the other researchers in the loop. This form can be used by a
research team in a variety of ways. In large projects, there should be an
understanding that the research will 'fund' many publications, some of which
will be authored by the entire team, and others, particularly if they are 'special
interest' publications, may be authored by smaller groups within the team.
Other research teams will agree to have all researchers named on all publications
with the order changing depending on who takes the lead managing and
writing the publication. This needs to be explicitly outlined by the research
team before a publication plan is established. Depending on how the publications
are being managed in the group, the PPF can be used for individual researchers,
when they have an idea for publication, to fill out and send it to the team. Other
members that are interested in, and have time to, help write the planned
publication can add their name and the publication can develop from there.

Beyond being useful for the internal administration of the research, the dissemination plan (in a modified form) can be included in the research application as it outlines how a team are planning to divide the research findings up for publication. You will notice that we have included research papers at conferences, academic papers in journals and scholarly books. For the sake of this chapter we have divided dissemination and communication under different subheadings. In reality, most research communication and dissemination plans will have publications for academic and other audiences in the same table. We discuss them separately in this chapter to provide a sense of the scope and the audiences for each type of publication. While plans obviously change, the kind of table presented in Table 10.1 provides evidence for funders that researchers have considered and integrated research dissemination and communication into their research plans. When it comes time to communicate your research to your academic peers there are several questions that can guide your dissemination strategy including:

- Who will be most interested in the findings of this research in my field?

- Are there researchers from other fields who will be interested in this research?

- What kinds of journals are publishing similar research?

- What is the academic standing and readership of the journal with which I am considering publication?

- Are there opportunities to publish the outcomes of the earlier part of the research including literature reviews and discussions relating to methodological strategies?

- Can the outcomes of the research be offered to different academic audiences such as adolescent psychology, childhood development, leisure sciences, sociology or anthropology?

Beyond these questions which you need to answer when you are developing a communication and dissemination plan, the other set of questions you need to ask yourself is what resources are available to you for the publication of the research. Research managers are often an invaluable resource at this stage of the research. As the research analysis and implementation phases are concluded they can concentrate on supporting the creation and implementation of the publication plan. At this stage research managers or research assistants recruited for the task can:

- develop the literature review for publication;

- identify key dates for the submission of drafts for discussion;

- maintain the dataset for publication;

- assist with the editing process;

- assist with the identification of journals for the work; and

- manage the revision and resubmission processes.

Making your research count

Before publishing, however, you must determine, with the help of your institution, what constitutes research for publication. Developing publications is difficult enough without realizing afterwards that the publications are not recognized for the purposes of research assessment. In your context the details will differ but many of the same criteria will apply. According to the Australian Government, for example, research comprises:

- Any activity classified as research that is characterized by originality; it should have investigation as a primary objective and should have the potential to produce results that are sufficiently general for humanity's stock of knowledge (theoretical and/or practical) to be recognizably increased. Most higher education research work would qualify as research.

- Pure basic research, strategic basic research, applied research and experimental development.

- Substantial scholarly activity, as evidenced by discussion of the relevant literature, an awareness of the history and antecedents of work described, and provided in a format which allows a reader to trace sources of the work, including through citations and footnotes.

- Originality (i.e. not a compilation of existing works) veracity/validity through a peer review process or by satisfying the commercial publisher processes.

- Increasing the stock of knowledge.

- Being in a form that enables dissemination of knowledge. (DEST 2012)

It is useful to be aware of the definitions of 'research' that your country and institution align with, to ensure that your publications of research findings are considered appropriately original, reliable and scholarly. We would like to consider now the different outlets for partnership research dissemination to the academic community.

Publishing in journals

The gold standard for publication in many disciplines such as educational psychology is publication in peer-reviewed journals. Or as Yates argues 'In University contexts, a pragmatic indicator of what good research looks like is that it is research that has been published in or is publishable in academic refereed journals' (Yates 2004: p. 85). While publishing in peer-reviewed journals can be time-consuming, it is not only a necessary feature of a successful academic career, but also an outlet for research dissemination often used by the academic community. When considering publishing in journals you should first determine that the audience for the journal fits with the kinds of article that will emerge from your research. You can determine this by reviewing the kinds of research and journals you have cited in your own literature review to see if they are still relevant for the kinds of research you have produced. In the last decade there has been a proliferation of journals that will consider and publish research findings from partnership researchers. Open access journals often provide exciting opportunities for publication. This proliferation of academic publication outlets also comes with its own dangers. When considering a journal for your work, assess its reputation in your field or the field in which you wish to publish and whether your peers consider it a valuable resource for their own research. Before you submit your article it may be useful to use a critical friend as described in Chapter 9 to assess the work and provide advice. We are not going to discuss here the processes for publication in peer-reviewed journals. The processes for review are well known and available on the websites of the journals you are considering. In essence Yates believes that good research reflected in journal articles 'addresses the agenda of that journal, takes account of what has gone before, and is seen to add to it' (Yates 2004: p. 104).

The academic book

Large-scale partnership research often provides the basis for excellent academic books. While journal articles allow researchers to focus on specific aspects of research, academic books, or monographs as they are sometimes known, allow researchers to reflect the comprehensiveness of a research project in all its holistic glory. There are several approaches to an academic book arising from partnership research. Partnership researchers can produce a single authored book, multiple authored book (like this one), or an edited book. For some projects it may be appropriate to do a combination of these, whereby part 1 is authored by the researchers, and part 2 is a series of edited chapters produced by the partners or participants. This is a particularly effective structure for design-based research studies. Table 10.2 provides a brief summary of the advantages and disadvantages of each approach.

Table 10.2 Advantages and disadvantages of publication by type

Type of publication	Sole authored book	Co-authored book	Edited book	Text book
Features	Control your own time frames Control your own vision Time consuming	All the advantages of teamwork All the disadvantages of teamwork Half or one third the effort depending on the number and responsibilities of the authors	Requires strong organization, administration and motivation skills Strong editorial teams can lessen the load Wikis or collaborative online spaces can be used to control the process Editing books carries little academic kudos	Recognized by some research education panels but not usually in education Usually a wide readership Can provide some royalty income

Before we discuss reasons to choose one or more of these approaches, we would like to consider reasons for publishing a book and what quality book-publication emerging from partnership research looks like. Nixon and Wellington (2005: p. 100) argue that: ' "good books" within the field of academic practice are imbued with the goods of that practice and of the academic traditions that carry forward that practice: the goods, for example, of attentiveness and sincerity, of explication and openness, of accuracy and honesty'.

Nixon and Wellington's point is that academic books should be reflective of the academic traditions and practices of their field. Researchers should not feel hamstrung by outmoded perceptions of what an academic book should look like. Technological advances in the publishing of books (and journals) have allowed the integration of research artefacts within publications in a commonplace way which should free the academic researcher to present the research in ways that are authentic and reflective of the research project. This means the integration of sound, video, etc. can now be considered when planning electronic publications. According to Yates's book publishers are seeking: 'Research that many people want to read about or that many libraries want to stock ... It is research writing where having something striking, useful or controversial to say is more important than having a detailed justification of approach and methodology. Creativity and skill in writing matters' (Yates 2004: p. 189).

When developing an academic book from research, your writing skills matter. Writing a book is not the same as a PhD thesis or an academic journal article, it must give a sense of the scope and range of the research in a way that engages the reader. The best kinds of academic books are similar to other kinds of books, they inspire, provoke and excite readers, and are of use to ongoing research. The highest compliment for an academic book is to discover that it has been cited or used by other researchers as the basis of further research. The questions that arise from your research are a key resource for future research in the area and should not be hidden or lost for the sake of interesting reading.

Let's now consider the different kinds of academic books in which partnership research can be presented. Depending on the scope of your research, it may be possible to present your work in several books. The *Fair Go* project (e.g. Munns, Zammit and Woodward 2008) has produced at least three different books for different audiences. We are not suggesting that there is a right way or type of book for your research. Where and in what ways you publish will depend on the experience and the skills of the research team and the nature of your research.

The role of the partner is also crucial in the publication process. Ordinarily there are protocols in the development and delivery of partnership research but often the publication of that research occurs after the research is complete. Many research contracts delineate a cut off for researchers to notify partners of any publications. There is, however, an issue of good faith here. In our view it is useful to keep the partner advised of the publications in a respectful way so that they can understand how the research continues to be communicated. While researchers are not often obliged to do this, it will support the ongoing relationship between the researcher and the partner. We are not suggesting here that the partner should have veto rights over the research but simply that the partner should be advised of the ongoing life of the research and its relevance to academic and non-academic audiences. It is important to be aware of the contractual agreements between partners and researchers with regard to publications as some partners will require veto rights and/or may have their own exclusive rights to publish elements of the research. For instance, in Case Study 5 (Chapter 5) as funders of the research, the Department of Education and Communities 'owned' the research outcomes. A specific agreement was reached at the beginning of the project regarding publication rights. As owners of the content, the DEC had exclusive rights to publish the Community Inquiry Framework, which was developed from the research findings as a DEC resource for teachers. Beyond this framework, however, the research team was able to publish the findings from the research in academic journals, conference proceedings and book chapters. The DEC required the research team to inform them of the upcoming publications and provide a copy of the publication prior to submission.

Approaching a publisher

Partnership researchers understand perhaps more than other researchers the need to create and maintain relationships. This understanding is beneficial when approaching publishers with book proposals. The first step, like the journal publication process, is to find publishers who are respected in the area of your research and have published similar work. When you have selected a shortlist of three or four publishers, search their website for a publication proposal form. These proposal forms differ from publisher to publisher but they all are similar questions that relate to market, the reputation of the authors, the need for the work, competing titles and sometimes a request for a simple piece of writing (usually a recent journal article or a chapter or two of the proposed work). In our experience, it is best to make a quick phone call or send a short email outlining in précis the idea behind your book before going to the trouble of developing the proposal. Before this phone call prepare by developing responses for the following questions that will be uppermost in the publisher's consideration of your work:

- What is the market?
- What is unique/novel/new about the work?
- What markets will it sell into? (Consider international markets as well)
- Why are you the person to write this book?

If at all possible find a series that your book could fit within and contact the series editors to see whether they are interested in including your book. This can have the effect of creating a shortcut between proposal and acceptance as the series editor will often be keen for new titles to include in the series and will expedite the approval processes. Series editors will often approach researchers and commission books for their series. If you have good contacts with publishers or series editors, start your enquiries with them. Building a good relationship with as publisher will mean that you will know quickly whether your work is of interest to them. In our experience publishers are usually happy to suggest other publishers who may be interested in your work if they can't use it in their list. Again, the key here is persistence. We have at times had to submit proposals numerous times they were accepted. It is normally a matter of responding to any criticism offered, refine your proposal and keep submitting it until you find a publisher who understands the need for your work.

The monograph (sole authored/co-authored)

In education, books are one of the primary ways for communicating research. The monograph is a good way to communicate large and complex ideas arising from comprehensive research projects. For the purposes of this discussion we are assuming that a monograph is a substantial piece of written work authored by one, two or three authors. Monographs are best suited to partnership research projects that have one or two chief investigators. In a small team a sole authored or co-authored book is less likely to lead to arguments about who contributes to what. The main advantage of the monograph is it allows authors to control the scope, timing and concepts of the book. The monograph is time-consuming for authors as it requires them to act as content editors and contributors all rolled into one. Monographs are, however, more prestigious than many other forms of publication. This does depend though on the field you are publishing in. Our colleagues in educational psychology for instance favour journal articles over academic books. Before you consider your publication strategy seek advice from your research institution and your colleagues about the most effective medium for the dissemination of your work.

Edited books

Edited books provide an opportunity for large groups of researchers to contribute to a collection of research that reflects a broad and complex research project. Edited books by teams of researchers offer ways to reflect several different facets of the research. While there needs to be cohesion in an edited book arising from the research, the content of an edited book does not need to cohere as strongly as a monograph. An edited book can accommodate different views and different perspectives on the same research and is ideal for a large and diverse group of researchers. When considering an edited book, one of the key issues will be who takes on the role of editor. Like many tasks in partnership research this role is best shared. Appointing one or two coordinating editors will ensure that this largely thankless task is completed with a minimum of fuss. Appointing an editor/s to oversee a publication such as this also provides a coherence to the text and will ensure a strong connection between the research and the final publication. Working with a large and geographically spread team on an edited book is made much easier through technological solutions such as online collaborative workspaces. Many collaborative research teams will have this kind of infrastructure already in place and be used to working with this approach. These online workspaces make the submission, editing and revision of work far more efficient. The *Fair Go* project based in Australia has recently produced a good example of an edited book arising from a partnership research project. *Exemplary Teachers of Students in Poverty* (Munns, Sawyer and Cole 2013) features fifteen chapters from members of the *Fair Go* research team. Any large partnership research project has a small army of researchers working on the project. In this instance, many of the researchers who were not necessarily the chief investigators were able to contribute to the publication as it related to their areas of interest in the project. In Box 10.2 we have included the description of this research as an exemplar of an edited book arising from a large research project. This book and others like it provide a model for partnership researchers considering publication outlets for their work. The editors describe the book in this way:

Box 10.2 Book description: *Exemplary Teachers of Students in Poverty*

Education and poverty exist in a highly contested relationship even in the developed world. On the one hand, educational outcomes seem solidly attached to socio-economic status, and on the other, education is often cited as a way out of poverty. Success at de-coupling poverty from educational outcomes varies across the developed world. The issues connecting education and poverty are complex, but the question of the successful engagement of students from poor backgrounds involves a complex mix of public policy on poverty, public policy on education, and teacher action. This book focuses on a number of exemplary teachers who demonstrate a set of common pedagogical qualities, assisting them to work productively with persistent classroom challenges in low SES classrooms.

EXEMPLARY TEACHERS OF STUDENTS IN POVERTY shares successful classroom practice from schools serving diverse and disadvantaged communities, and stresses that opportunities in school can influence educational engagement and encourage students to achieve. The text locates itself in international debates about education and poverty, and reports on the Teachers for a Fair Go project – an Australian research project into the work of a number of teachers who were successful at engaging students from poor backgrounds.

Included in the book:

- teaching in low SES communities
- what exemplary teachers of students in low SES communities do
- specific pedagogical approaches in literacy, ICT, creativity and culturally responsive practices
- students' voices
- professional qualities of these teachers

EXEMPLARY TEACHERS OF STUDENTS IN POVERTY will greatly benefit researchers, teacher-educators and trainee teachers, allowing them to gain a much deeper understanding of the issues, constraints and perspectives in teaching contexts across low SES communities. (Munns, Sawyer and Cole 2013)

There are many other ways that you can publish your work to academic audiences. We have not considered the opportunities of publishing through conference proceedings nor have we considered creative works as avenues for the dissemination of partnership research. The types of places you publish your work will be entirely dependent on your project, your partner and the audience you are trying to reach. Whatever the case, planning for publication at the application stage of your proposal is the most efficient way to ensure that publications will happen as a result of the project. In the next section we turn our discussion to communicating the outcomes of the research with partnership organizations.

Communicating with partner organizations

One of the primary responsibilities of having a partner in research is to keep them in the loop throughout the research. Involving them in the research will have several benefits and will ensure that your research project remains relevant to their needs. When it comes time to deliver your findings this communication becomes critical. It is at this moment that partners will decide whether the research you have developed is worthwhile and applicable to them and can potentially affect your ongoing relationship with that partner. Our advice is to plan this communication strategy well ahead of completing your research. It is wise to begin the discussions about how research will be communicated to the research partner at least twelve months in advance of completing the research. You should have been providing the partner with interim updates throughout the research to create a culture of information sharing between the partner and the research team. When you are planning for the final dissemination of your research project there are several strategies you can employee to ensure the organization feels enriched, supported and enhanced by the research. In the next section of this chapter we would like to discuss several approaches to communicating with your partner. These strategies can be presented to a partner in the planning phases of the research to fit their needs. The best strategy is to consider a suite of presentations that include information sharing, capacity building, and detailed planning and support arising from the partnership research project. When you are developing a partnership communication strategy the following questions may assist:

- What does the partner need to know about the research?
- Are there different audiences within partner organizations that need to know about different aspects of the research?
- Are there opportunities for the partner to showcase their research to others in the industry?
- Are there opportunities to brief senior management in partner organizations?

- Are there opportunities to brief senior policymakers/bureaucrats or politicians about the outcomes of the research?

- Are there elements of the research that the partner does not want to profile?

- Are the elements of the research that the partner particularly wants to profile?

Written report

A standard feature of most partnership research is the formal report presented to a partner at the end of the research. This report is unlike a research report as it focuses on and emphasizes the aspects of the research that can be readily applied to the partner's needs. Before presenting the partner with a report of this type, ensure that you understand what the partner's expectations are. In our experience partners are not likely to want a report that extends beyond twenty pages. If it is necessary to write a longer report then a detailed summary of key findings is often useful for partner organizations to use to share the work. If you have multiple partners, you may need to develop a report for each partner. Where there are multiple partners there are often sensitivities around sharing information between partners. If you intend to share information between partners, ensure that you have permission from each partner to do so. A report of this kind might have the following subheadings:

- executive summary/abstract

- background to the research

- methods used in the research

- findings of the research

- conclusions and recommendations

These suggested content areas will change from partner to partner. It may be useful to ask the partner for a research report they have received in the past which they found useful. This can be used as a model for communicating with the partner in a formal research report. The main interest for the partner will relate directly to how they can apply the outcomes of the research to make their organizations practice and policy more effective.

Presentation

It is not unusual when presenting research findings to a partner to be asked to give a presentation. The challenge, however, is to create a presentation that will be noticed by the partner. The usual 'death by PowerPoint' should be avoided when developing and delivering a presentation on your research. Our suggestion is that you use video, images and graphics as much as possible and keep the findings and recommendations simple, relevant and direct. Remember that many of the people attending these presentations do not have the depth of understanding that the research team and key players in the partner organization have in this research. Approach these presentations assuming little knowledge of the project. In essence, what attendees for these presentations want to know is 'so what?' They want to know how the research is relevant to them and how it can impact on their practice to make what they do more effective. Recently, we presented research to teachers. The teachers in this session wanted to know how our findings derived from classroom research could help them be better teachers. They were not particularly interested in the minutiae of the research project. They wanted to know quickly and clearly what the implications of the research were for them.

Some partners will ask you to provide a presentation for senior management. Ordinarily you will only get ten to fifteen minutes to get your point across to people at this level. Obviously these people are very busy and they to want you to 'cut to the chase'. Developing five key points for these kinds of presentations that reflect the relevance and the ongoing impact of the research on the organization's performance is more likely to be successful than a longer presentation that provides more detail. In essence, these presentations need to be short, sharp and clear for their audience. If you are able to include a member of the partner organization in these presentations this can be a powerful strategy to improve the perceived relevance of the research.

Workshop

Many organizations ask for partnership researchers to develop capacity through professional learning workshops. In these workshops the research findings are presented and members of the partnership organization are given the opportunity to apply these research findings directly to their work. These workshops can last from between two hours to two days. Recently, we were invited to assist a large non-government organization that we were partnering with to develop a half-day workshop on evaluation strategies in sensitive communities. We developed a programme that introduced the research and then asked participants to consider the findings in the light of their area of responsibility. The second session introduced them to innovative of evaluation strategies, and asked them to consider how they could apply these to their own area. In the third session the participants were asked to develop an evaluation strategy for their own programmes. These kinds of workshops are a 'value add' for partnership organizations as they bring the skills of the researcher, the findings of the research and the applied knowledge of the partner together to develop capacity within the organization. These workshops are usually only possible if you have a good relationship with the partner and they are convinced that your research is useful, applicable and has ongoing relevance for the organization.

Other forms of presentation

There are several other forms of presentation available to partnership researchers. For instance, we were recently asked to develop a short film that outlined the research we had developed and the findings of that research for partnership organization. This short film (five minutes long) was sent throughout the organization, nationally and internationally. We are aware of several other approaches for partners including the development and staging of a play, an art exhibition and an installation. While some of these approaches may sound unconventional they suited the needs of the partner and the researchers.

Another approach we have seen work well is providing high-level consultancy in the ongoing planning of the partnership organization. While this is not a common occurrence for communicating results, it does indicate that the partners are taking the research seriously and are determined to use the research to bring change to the organization. In these situations researchers are invited to assist senior management to provide evidence-based strategies for the ongoing efficiency and reform of the organization. Researchers should strive to confine their advice in this situation to the outcomes of the research.

Community communication strategies

While communicating research findings to partner organizations is a central part of partnership research, the broader community is a major stakeholder in many partnership research projects, particularly those achieved through government funding. A responsibility that accompanies this funding is to make the research broadly available to others within the community to whom it may be relevant. Many researchers refer to their media performances as evidence of the impact of their research. While this is only partially true, the media does provide one opportunity to communicate the findings of research to a broader public. There are many academics that are reluctant to engage with the media fearing that the complexity of their research will be 'dumbed down'. This is a valid fear. Research projects are routinely complex, often ambiguous and sometimes difficult to share with non-specialists. On the other hand, there is a great deal that can be gained from sharing the outcomes of research with the community at large. In this section of this chapter we would like to suggest some strategies for communicating the outcomes of partnership research projects with the broader community. The communication of partnership research to the broader community also has some sensitivities for the partners and the researchers. These sensitivities can be managed effectively with some planning. Putting processes in place ensures the needs of the partner and the needs of the researchers are both met.

Sharing partnership research with the community

Firstly, it is often appropriate to ensure that the partner organization/s are a central part of a public communication strategy for the research and that the credit for the research is shared amongst all the institutions involved. Many partners have a dedicated media management capacity that can assist you to develop a media strategy that suits the needs of the partner and the needs of the research institution. A joint strategy is often developed collaboratively between media officers within the research institution and the partner organization. Medical research institutes and hospitals often develop media releases and host media conferences to share the outcomes of research. These joint strategies are commonplace and most media offices in large partners will have several precedent experiences to draw from when developing these kinds of strategies. Problems can arise when researchers do not consult the partners to ensure they are happy for the outcomes of the research to be shared. The untimely release of research information can cause political and sometimes ethical difficulties in some partner organizations. Before we explore the specific channels for communicating with the community, let's discuss some specific approaches to communicating research to a broader audience. The following are some guidelines we have developed through our own experience of trying to share our work with the broader community.

Make sometimes complex ideas and arguments simple

In most cases those interested enough in your research to read an article or listen to radio a report on it will not have much time to digest great amounts of complexity. While we might want it to be otherwise, the reality is we have a very short amount of space or time to communicate the 'so what?' of our research. Most research projects of any scale have a public-facing website that can support those interested in more detail on the research. Perhaps the best we can hope for when communicating through the media is a short amount of information that tells the reader or listener what's distinctive and relevant about the research for their lives. Keeping the message simple will ensure that journalists see the relevance of the work for the audience and are attracted to it. Cutting out jargon, highly complex theoretical discussion, and methodological discussions will clarify and reduce your message to a form that is palatable to a broad audience. There are, of course, exceptions. Many specialist programmes have the time and ability to explore some of the research you have developed in great depth. For the mainstream non-specialist media, however, three or four points about the relevance of the research to the imagined audience is sufficient. Any reader or listener who is interested in pursuing it further can do so in greater depth through your research papers that can be posted on your more detailed website.

Relate your project to news worthy items

The media works in cycles that relate to newsworthy items. These cycles can last from between two or three hours to three weeks depending on the newsworthiness of the story. Medical researchers are adept at sensing what is newsworthy and working their research into a media cycle. It may be worth considering waiting for one or two weeks until a topic of general relevance appears in the news and linking your research to that item. If your research is of passing interest only to the media this strategy will make your chances of getting coverage much higher. So for instance, if your research relates to reading patterns in early childhood learning it is more likely that your research will be covered when there are news stories around about early childhood learning or childcare shortages. This is not to suggest that stories will not be picked up out of the media cycle but this approach will improve your chances of getting a public audience for your research. The media professionals in your organizations can provide advice on this aspect of media coverage.

Tell the story of the research

Developing ways of speaking about your research as a narrative can provide strong points of connection for the community. Research projects often have compelling stories that relate to the way they began and key moments collected through the research. These stories do not need to reflect the entirety of the research but rather they need to reflect some of the messages that emerge from the research. For instance, in the TheatreSpace research many young people who attended the theatre reported in interviews the highly influential role of the family in their developing engagement with performance. One young person described the thrill of sitting on her grandfather's knee while she watched performance of Shakespeare's *A Midsummer Night's Dream*. In media interviews, we related this vignette emerging from the research to communicate a message relating to the importance of the family in developing theatre attendance patterns. This vignette was the metaphorical tip of the iceberg and we had comprehensive data to back up our finding about the relationship between the family and theatre attendance. The story, however, gave us the opportunity to communicate a narrative from our research that has the potential to engage the interest of a broader audience. We had several narratives emerging from the major findings of the research and we tailored our communication to the audiences that we were trying to reach.

Justify and promote your research

Beyond the altruistic reasons for sharing your research we have provided here there are some that relate directly to academic career paths and opportunities for ongoing research. Media coverage of partnership research that features partners signals to other potential partners that your research has been relevant and beneficial. Media coverage such as this can encourage those considering research to contact you; it identifies you as a researcher with interests and a capacity in education research. This kind of coverage also identifies you and your team as a group of people who can work in partnership on applied research projects. These kinds of media placements will build your reputation as a dependable researcher who can create projects that deliver outcomes for partners that are of relevance to the community. PhD students are often recruited through this kind of research and this kind of media coverage is often prized in universities by Deans and Vice Chancellors. Of course, this is not the only reason to undertake this kind of coverage; it does, however, allow you to position yourself as a trusted partnership researcher.

Conclusion

In some senses research projects are not fully completed until their outcomes are communicated and disseminated to the wider world. Communication and dissemination strategies are sometimes one of the last considered pieces of research. They are, however, crucial in discharging your responsibility to your partner, your research institution and the broader community. Academics who publish are less likely, as the old saying goes, to 'perish'. However, publication in partnership research demands that we think creatively and strategically in conjunction with the partner about the most useful places and spaces for our findings to prove the relevance. Partnership researchers can support partnership organizations in becoming research responsive by thinking carefully and planning effectively the ways the research can be used to support capacity building and reform in their partner organizations. Some researchers are reluctant to engage beyond this point with the media for fear of demeaning their research. This fundamentally misunderstands the role of the media in the research communication process. The media provides an opportunity for researchers to get three or four key messages across that relate directly to the relevance of their research and the impact of that research for the community more generally. While avoiding the media is possible, this avoidance also denies the community at large the benefits of the research they are ultimately stakeholders in.

Partnership researchers need to consider in the very early stages of their project strategies that will meet the needs of the partner, the research institutions, and the community more generally. The channels and opportunities for communication have multiplied exponentially in the last decade. There is now no excuse for research not finding an audience. Now there are also many different strategies for communicating to each audience. It is up to researchers and their partners to find ways of communicating that allow the knowledge that has been created as part of the research to be transferred for the benefit of institutional and non-institutional audiences.

The next chapter draws the book to a close with some final reflections on the future of partnership research and some concluding thoughts about how educational researchers can maximize research relationships with partners.

Key messages from the chapter

- Partnership researchers have a particular responsibility to share the findings from their research. In education, research is taken seriously by many policymakers and practitioners when developing programmes and policy that influence learning in education settings.

- Researchers have a responsibility that comes with research funding to provide the benefits of that research to those who have funded it. In a majority of cases those funders are governments and therefore the community through their taxes.

- Intellectual property can be a divisive issue on partnership projects. Putting clear publication plans in place, which have been discussed and agreed upon by members of the research team and the partner organizations, can have the effect of avoiding these kinds of divisions.

- A Publication Dissemination Plan is useful for the internal administration of the research and can be included in the research application as it outlines how a team are planning to divide up the research findings for publication.

- While publishing in peer-reviewed journals can be time-consuming, it is not only a necessary feature of a successful academic career, but also an outlet for research dissemination often used by the academic community.

- There are several approaches to an academic book arising from partnership research. Partnership researchers can produce a single authored book, multiple authored books, an edited book or all of these.

- There are also now many different strategies for communicating to each audience. It is up to researchers and their partners to find ways of communicating that allow the knowledge that has been created as part of the research to be transferred for the benefit of institutional and non-institutional audiences.

CHAPTER ELEVEN

Reflections on the way ahead for partnership research

At the beginning of this book we explained why we think partnership research in education matters. Throughout the book, we have endeavoured to provide 'real-world' discussions about how partnership research can be undertaken effectively, and through case studies have given evidence of the impact that well planned and executed partnership research can have on our field. In this concluding chapter we would like to revisit some of the original ideas about 'making knowledge matter' and consider some of the 'what ifs' of partnership research. In essence, we dig into the realities and unmet potentialities of this kind of approach to research. In the course of the discussion we will pick up on some of the themes that have featured in this book to identify what the future opportunities might be for researchers, partners, schools and communities if we manage to create and execute partnership research effectively.

Why partnership research is here to stay

In education, there is a tendency towards practice. It is, after all, the focus of most teachers' work. Therefore, for many researchers who have been teachers and continued teaching at university, practice is top of mind when considering educational issues. The proliferation of partnership research granting schemes amongst national funding bodies also indicates that governments see partnership research as an area that is critical to the development and sustainability of sectors such as education. Partnership researchers and the projects they produce are required because practice needs to continue to change in response to dynamic and shifting conditions in society. Consider the changes that have been brought to classrooms and other places of learning by the rapid and evolving possibilities of technology. These changes have implications for the way students learn, the way learners interact with each other and their development as citizens in a changing community. These changes require researchers with skills and experience that can locate their research in practice and are able to build evidence to support the ongoing growth and enhancement of learning and teaching practice, policy and theory in a rapidly changing world. These changes will create a demand for researchers who can negotiate the often difficult terrain of partnership research and who understand the dynamic nature of learning and teaching.

Our examination of partnership research here and our strong advocacy for it is not meant to suggest that those doing research which is not partnership focused is in any way inferior to the partnership research discussed in this book. The research community needs all kinds of researchers and we would be much the poorer if researchers working in other ways were not an integral part of the research landscape. We do, however, need to create and propagate a clear rationale for ongoing partnership research that is effectively funded and thoughtfully sustained to ensure that the evidence base for changes in practice in education is supported.

We wish to spend some time in this conclusion reflecting on the ways this might be achieved. Our reflections here are the results of our experience in partnership research, including our frustrations and our aspirations but also our own perspectives regarding the ways research is changing. In the same ways that the teaching practice that partnership researchers examined is changing, research as a practice is also being altered by similar and in some cases the same forces. In compiling the next section of this chapter we are speculating about what could make partnership research stronger, more effective – and critically – more relevant for teachers and students in schools and other sites where learning and teaching takes place. We have organized our speculative recommendations into reasonably arbitrary subheadings and we recognize that all of the factors we identify here interact and overlap in complex ways. They are an attempt to speculate about what we see as the barriers to effective practice in partnership research at the moment and contemplate the possible reforms and changes that could make partnership research more achievable and more effective.

Partnership research practice – some problems and speculative solutions

Given the prevalence of partnership research, it is stunning in some ways that this is one of the first books that deals explicitly with practices in this area. Perhaps it is the case that researchers have considered partnership research to be not particularly 'special' or unique. While in some ways this might be true, there are particular skills and abilities that make partnership research possible and effective. The skills we have discussed throughout this book that relate to; relationships, networks, systems and the management of all of the complex features of partnership research require special attention. Our discussions here are an attempt to raise the profile of partnership research as an area that requires support from granting organizations, institutions such as universities and partners so that partnership research can thrive in an often competitive research environment.

One avenue for such support is through focused research training that understands and responds to the needs of partnerships. Most partnership researchers get their initial training in research through research higher-degree courses. To our knowledge, there are no specific training programmes in research that deal with the dynamics, complexities and intricacies of researching with partners. Certainly, in our own experiences as PhD students there was nothing available to us in our research training coursework that prepared us for the demands of partnership research. Instead, this was considered to be learnt 'on the job'. While experience can be a powerful teacher, PhD research experiences are not always targeted effectively to develop the skills required to build a career as a partnership researcher in education. This differs substantially from other areas of academic life. Biologists who do their research training in laboratories learn the protocols and approaches required to be successful in that environment. While of course research sites will change, biologists can expect that laboratory sites will be a large part of their research. Education researchers do not, however, work in a predictable environment – making the education researcher's job more challenging in some respects. While we acknowledge that no training could ever hope to cover the range and diversity of sites that partnership researchers will encounter throughout their career, there are common sets of skills and understandings (we examined many of these in this book) that will prepare partnership researchers for the field. Training that relates to relationship building, team management, building critical networks and research communication could be of substantial benefit to researchers contemplating this career path.

Beyond disciplines and fields – the possibility of interdisciplinary research

One avenue that has not been explored in detail in this volume, yet has both a central and complex relationship to partnership research, is interdisciplinary research. Making interdisciplinary research possible and attractive is another way to support and boost partnership research for institutions such as universities and granting organizations. We suggest this research is made 'attractive' to researchers because, notwithstanding various universities rhetorical positions on the value of interdisciplinary research, there are persistent and sometimes insoluble barriers for researchers who want to work between and across silos. There are, of course, good examples of partnership education research projects that are interdisciplinary. They tend to be the exception rather than the rule. The faculty system in universities has many benefits, but in our experience it fosters territoriality that diminishes the opportunities for collaboration across fields. Many of the successful interdisciplinary research projects that we know of have been made possible by the seniority of the lead researcher who comes to the research with an established reputation that can be used as a kind of 'research capital' to bring in researchers from other areas. Early career and mid-career researchers rarely have this research capital to bargain with and are left to work within their own field to create research. As we all know, knowledge cannot be siloed into arbitrary faculty-based systems of understanding and yet many universities continue to pretend that it can be. In an age of ubiquitous and free-flowing knowledge (made possible through rapid advances in technology) it must be time for us to rethink the way knowledge and knowledge creators are organized in places like universities. A fundamental rethinking of the way researchers are organized, housed and separated may make interdisciplinary partnership research teams the norm rather than the exception and reduce inefficient overlaps and duplication of effort.

Internationalizing research

Another way of breaking down the siloed nature of knowledge is to consider the potential of international research partnerships as the norm rather than the exception. Typically, partnership research is carried out on a national basis with teams drawn from the partner and local researchers. This makes sense for many partnership research projects. There are, however, several projects that would benefit from being carried out across national borders. Assuming a deeper relevance or connection with partners according to how geography is, at times, arbitrary. It may be that there are deeper resonances with those working in similar fields, or working with similar communities overseas. While the tyranny of distance can make coordination and logistics difficult for this kind of research, the affordances of technology has made these tyrannies far less daunting. For instance, in a recent project on using technology (such as motion sensor and virtual reality games technologies) to teach classical texts (*Macbeth*) the research leader (chief investigator), based in the UK developed a programme of research that was housed in the UK but also had parallel research undertaken (on a smaller scale) in the United States, the UK and Australia. The research project that partnered libraries and theatre companies investigated the research question ('how do you engage young people with classical texts?') has international relevance and appeal. While each context has different features, this project benefited from bringing these diverse international perspectives to bear on the research question. The global nature of classical texts, video games, and learning means that the outcomes of the research could be made global because of the internationalized nature of the study. This kind of partnership research insulates projects from being captives of their own context yet still allow researchers to take account and be perceptive to these local contexts. This approach will not suit every partnership research project. Many projects are context specific and make sense as a local or national project. There are, however, several opportunities in partnership research that have not always been realized because partnership researchers have not had the international networks nor the understanding of the potential for international research.

Internationalizing partnership research is by no means an easy feat, which is perhaps the real reason why it happens less regularly. There are institutional, national and even international disincentives to working collaboratively across borders, whether they are universities, states or nations. While there have been some attempts to make international research more appealing and achievable these have until now been exceptional. Reform is required in both policy and practice so research councils can assist researchers to fully maximize the opportunities in developing these kinds of collaborations by making funding easier to access for researchers working in this way. A further, and we think necessary, step is to mandate a certain portion of partnership research that is internationally collaborative in nature. These kinds of reforms would have significant downstream benefits to researchers and their stakeholders reducing the sometimes pointless barriers faced by researchers who are working internationally, between and across disciplines.

Using technology to make research possible

We have touched on what might be possible using the technological tools available in research. There are however, further opportunities to extend the reach of partnership research through the employment of technology on a more widespread basis. There are many opportunities for partnership researchers to use technology to make their practice more efficient. Recently, researchers have been funding their research through crowdfunding. Crowdfunding is a way to raise finances for research by using several small donations to provide sufficient funds for usually small scale but sometimes larger research projects. Sites on the Internet such as *Pozible* pitch the idea (in this case the research need) to an international audience (the crowd) to fund research. On the face of it this approach has many advantages. If you are working in partnership research, many of the areas you are researching will have some popular appeal. For instance, research on creating opportunities for disadvantaged students in schooling could potentially have appeal to national and international donors. Unlike other approaches that source funding from donors, crowdfunding can aggregate several small donations into larger sums that can make research possible. Researchers in science seem to have stolen the march on this approach to funding. Science crowdfunding sites such as *microaryza* provide researchers with a place to showcase their research and attract funding for it. This site provides potential funders with details about the research and offers updates throughout the progress of the research. These sites are typically well organized, well designed and integrate high-quality graphics and video to describe to potential donors the need for the research. These sites seem to specialize in small research projects of around $5,000–20,000 in size.

Crowdfunding will not be right for all research projects, but in some cases where the research has popular appeal and is modest in resources. It may fill a gap for early career researchers between small grants emanating from the university and the often elusive large external competitive grant. Even though science and health seem to be leading the way in this approach to funding, there is no reason why education could not develop similar methods for attracting research funding. In some ways crowdsourcing is a natural fit for researchers interested in partnering with the community to fund their research. Similar to crowdfunding, crowdsourcing of research collects research materials from the broadest possible audience. The approach can be useful when researchers are considering large populations and require feedback from a self-selected sample. There are many ethical and logistical issues with these kinds of approaches to funding and research. We have no doubt, however, that they will become a more established part of the research landscape over time as government resources for research shrinks and researchers search for ways to fund and deliver their work.

Funding

The various partnership research schemes around the world have been reduced and remodelled in response to the most recent financial crisis. Financial crises come and go and in a career of any length researchers will see good times and bad times for funding. Quite apart from these cycles, partnership researchers need to justify a special place and prosecute an argument for partnership research in the funding mix. We are not arguing for partnership research at the expense of other forms of research, but rather we are asserting that partnership research has special challenges, unique skills and particular funding needs. In our view, the partnership schemes that have been a feature of research funding for the last two decades have generally supported partnership research. In many countries, education has been the 'poor cousin' in the funding carve up. It is hard to determine why this is the case but we suspect that it is because the funding of partnership research is prone to the winds of political preference. Sometimes funding for a politically 'sexy' topic will take precedence over what policymakers, practitioners and researchers might consider as a more pressing need. There is recent evidence that politicians are very active in the selection and the vetoing of partnership research projects and in our view this politicization of the process is unfortunate. We think it is time to make research funding processes at arm's-length from political processes. While politicians have a role in setting policy, research-funding decisions should be made by those who will be the recipients of that research – the teachers, the policymakers, the school leaders and the students in schools. This may seem like a radical proposal but it is attempting to reconcile research funding with the partnership principles we have espoused throughout this book. For those in education to have confidence in research we must also have a funding regime that is free of interference and perceived bias. We must also have an equitable share of the 'research funding cake' to ensure partnership research in education remains viable and possible, and our stakeholders have a say in the research created for and with them.

Ending the practice/theory divide

One of the criterion that has often been used to create a distinction between partnership research and other research is the integration of theory into research. We believe the 'theory/practice divide' (Korthagen and Kessels 1999: p. 4) is another unhelpful dichotomy. Partnership researchers are as responsible for the creation and dissemination of theory as any other kind of researcher. In fact, as we discussed in Chapter 1, the unique potential for partnership research to inform multiple layers of the education field places a special responsibility on partnership researchers. At its core, partnership research in education researches education practice. Theory in education does not sit in splendid isolation, rather it has an essential and intimate relationship with the way practice and policy is shaped and changed. The practice/theory nexus in our view is essential to partnership research having a life beyond its own milieu and should be a component in the application for funding and the design of partnership research. It demonstrates that our research has gravity and applicability in several contexts and on several levels and legitimizes the role of partnership research in terms of its contribution to theoretical developments and debates.

End to methodological hierarchies

We have discussed in this book the futility of silos. While institutions often create silos for us, researchers have also had a role in creating pointless demarcations in the past relating to methodologies. Classically in education the fault lines have emerged between qualitative and quantitative research. While some methodological debate is healthy in any field, the tendency by some to exclude one methodology or another is pointless, and appears to us to simply limit the different ways we could find out more about what we do and how we can do it better. Most recently, the politics of 'evidence-based' research has seen a resurgence of this kind of discussion where one methodology is preferred above another for its ability to deliver 'evidence'. Partnership researchers into the future are likely to need many kinds of research to meet diverse research needs. No *one* methodology or type of methodology can meet the complex and diverse needs that emerge in partnership education research. We are not suggesting here that methodology is not important – it is. Being methodologically trained and aware is central for any researcher. What we are saying is perhaps rather than considering the method first and the question second, partnership researchers should begin with the research challenge and recruit methodologies and research teams to meet that need. This approach, which has been present on most of the partnership research projects we have been involved with, avoids pointless arguments about which methodology is better than which other methodology. The question in our view is which methodology is better for what question and how can methodologies be arranged in such a way to meet the needs of the project. The generation and presentation of evidence is far more sophisticated than it used to be. The challenge for partnership researchers is to argue for a more nuanced and sophisticated understanding of what evidence might mean in education research.

Communication and dissemination

One of the key and partially unmet challenges for partnership researchers is the communication of their research to diverse audiences. While researchers are often adept at communicating with their peers through journals and academic conferences there is still much to do in considering how we might share the benefits of partnership research with those who principally fund research; the community. Again, technology provides some opportunities to make research findings available to those who have an interest in the research. One of the projects that had good success with research communication was the TheatreSpace project (see Case Study 2, Chapter 2). This success was partly due to the integration of the communication strategy into the initial research design. The sheer number of partners (thirteen in all) meant that keeping them in the loop was always going to be a significant challenge. The project included an interim report that was delivered directly to the partners and a symposium that brought the research team and the partners together to discuss the research and its application in their organizations. Beyond the partners there is a responsibility to communicate the research findings to a public audience. The development of publicly available reports with a video to accompany and contextualize the findings was one way that the TheatreSpace project attempted to meet its commitment to making the findings of the report public.

On the horizon, there are some exciting opportunities for communicating research. Performance ethnography is one approach that incorporates the text of research participants in the scripting of a performance for stage or film. The intent of this approach is to 'dramatize the data' (Anderson and Wilkinson 2007). This approach recognizes that we have become an information-rich but time-poor society. While there is much research data available in printed form the fight for attention means that researchers will need to find more innovative ways to get their research into the public eye. This approach pushes research dissemination beyond 'academics talking to each other' and attempts to return the outcomes of the research directly to the audiences that it was sourced from. Typically, performances are created from the data and then taken back to the communities where the research was generated so that those communities can have the findings reflected back to them. Not all communities will want or need this but these kinds of communication approaches do signify and exemplify an attempt to reconnect research with the communities that provided the inspiration for that research to occur in the first place. This is a welcome change in the research landscape that suggests researchers are engaging in larger numbers with the challenge of communicating research to wider audiences. Hopefully performance ethnography and approaches like it will not be isolated. We hope that these approaches to communicating research will become more widespread as researchers realize the benefits in demonstrating the efficacy of their research to the communities that have provided the data for that research.

Exemplary partnership research

At the conclusion of this book we thought it might be useful to outline what we believe to be an exemplary instance of partnership research that has made an impact across various fields, included education. The Pathways to Resilience project began in Canada in 2007, funded by the National Crime Prevention Centre, and received further funding from the Social Sciences and Humanities Research Council of Canada (SSHRC), the International Development Research Centre and the Canadian Institutes of Health Research (CIHR), to continue to 2014. This research has been influential in developments relating to theory, practice and policy around youth, schooling, community development and resilience. It has also managed to connect with researchers in a multidisciplinary fashion beyond national borders and has created change for young people, families and schools. In short, this is a partnership research project that has created knowledge that matters to various disciplines, school systems and far beyond.

The Pathways to Resilience project has fourteen lead investigators, including Michael Ungar, the principal investigator, across five countries – Canada, China, Columbia, New Zealand, and South Africa. The project partners with communities and service providers in each of these countries to help them identify and understand:

- aspects of resilience that young people in their community use to cope with problems;

- risks that young people in their community face; and

- the extent and ways in which young people use services in the community, particularly mandated services (such as corrective services or child welfare) and informal support services in the community.

The team talk about their hope to provide:

> participating communities, schools, governments, and service providers with a very detailed understanding of young people's ways of coping with adversity and the risks they face. We would also like to help service providers from many different organizations find ways to coordinate services, create new services young people say they need, and find ways young people can engage with community and family supports that can help them 'grow up well' despite the challenges they face. (Ungar 2013)

The partnerships forged by this project are impressive, as are the different dissemination opportunities incorporated into the project (including a YouTube video, multiple academic journal articles and conference presentations, and to date, seventeen 'state of the nation' reports to the governments of the countries involved).

Extending the notion of partnership beyond the single study, however, this project is one of many being undertaken through the Resilience Research Centre (RRC). This research centre is a great example of how strong partnerships work. It brings together academic researchers from six continents (North America, Latin America, Europe, Africa, Asia and Australasia) and uses methodologically diverse approaches to study questions surrounding the core interest – youth resilience. Specifically,

> how children, youth, and families cope with many different kinds of adversity . . . The research we do is looking beyond individual factors to aspects of a young person's family, neighbourhood, wider community, school, culture, and the political and economic forces that exert an influence on a child's development in challenging contexts.
> (Resilience Research Centre 2013)

At the moment, the RRC partners with twenty-nine universities, seven other research centres, UNESCO, The World Bank, numerous charities (including the Red Cross) and has received funding from numerous government, philanthropic and research organizations. This concentration of researchers, funders, policy development organizations, and partners, has allowed for an effective and innovative, international, interdisciplinary and in-depth understanding of issues regarding youth resilience and well-being. Working together for a common interest, researchers have been able to share work, co-publish, become involved, and increase their understanding of the ways that resilience is related to a variety of disciplines, and how these fields intersect and connect around this critical issue.

Policy, practice and partnership research: Solving the disconnect

The real potential and raison d'être for partnership research is to close the gap between research, policy and practice. This is a challenge that partnership researchers have met with differing levels of success. The case studies that we have presented and the example from the Resilience Research Centre demonstrate that it is possible for partnership research, when planned carefully and delivered effectively, to create sustainable connections between research, policy and practice. Partnership research has a key role to play in connecting worlds that can become so easily disconnected and to create relevant, timely and influential understanding that directly meet the needs of education and makes knowledge that matters.

BIBLIOGRAPHY

Adler, P. A. and Adler, P. (1987), *Membership Roles in Field Research*. Qualitative Research Methods Series 6. Thousand Oaks, CA: Sage.

Anderson, M. and Freebody, K. (2012), 'Developing Communities of Praxis: Bridging the Theory/Practice Divide in Teacher Education', *McGill Journal of Education*, 47: 359–78.

Anderson, M. and O'Connor, P. (2013), 'Applied Theatre as Research: Provoking the Possibilities', *Applied Theatre Research*, 1(2): 189–202.

Anderson, M. and Wilkinson, L. (2007), 'A Resurgence of Verbatim Theatre: Authenticity, Empathy and Transformation', *Australasian Drama Studies*, (50): 153–69.

Australian Government (2013), *ARC Open Access Policy*. http://www.arc.gov.au/pdf/ARC%20Open%20Access%20Policy_print_version.pdf [Accessed 07 May 2013].

Bannan-Ritland, R. (2008), 'Teacher Design Research: An Emerging Paradigm for Teacher Professional Development', in A. E. Kelly, R. Leash and J. Y. Back (eds), *Handbook of Design Research Methods in Education*. New York: Routledge.

Barab, S. A., Barnett, M. G., and Squire, K. (2002), 'Developing an Empirical Account of a Community of Practice: Characterizing the Essential Tensions', *The Journal of the Learning Sciences*, 11(4): 489–542.

Barnett, R. (2000), 'Supercomplexity and the Curriculum', *Studies in Higher Education*, 25(3): 255–65.

Beattie, M. (1995), *Constructing Professional Knowledge in Teaching: A Narrative of Change and Development*. New York: Teachers College Press.

Boal, A. (1979), *Theatre of the Oppressed*. London: Pluto Press.

Bonne, L., Pritchard, R., Gault, S., Hendry, V., Holland, P., Kissling, G., Kliffen, S., Kyne, M., Miller, C. and Treeby, J. (2007), *Teachers Developing as Researchers: Teachers Investigate Their Use of Questions in Mathematics*. Teaching and Learning Research Initiative. http://www.tlri.org.nz/projects/2005/classroomquestioning.html [Accessed 16 October 2008].

Borko, H., Whitcomb, J. A. and Byrnes, K. (2008), 'Genres of Research in Teacher Education', in M. Cochran-Smith, S. Felman-Nemser and D. J. McIntyre (eds), *Handbook of Research on Teacher Education*, 3rd edn. New York: Routledge.

Bottrell, D. (2011), 'Shifting Perspectives, Representations and Dilemmas in Work with Young People', in A. Campbell and P. Broadhead (eds), *Working with Children and Young People: Ethical Debates and Practices Across Disciplines and Continents*. Oxford: Peter Lang.

Boydell, K. M., Volpe, T., Cox, S., Katz, A., Dow, R., Brunger, F., Parsons, J., Belliveau, G., Gladstone, B., Zlotnik-Shaul, R., Kamensek, O., Lafrenière, D. and Wong, L. (2012), 'Ethical Challenges in Arts-Based Health Research',

International Journal for the Creative Arts in Interdisciplinary Practice, (11): 1–17. http://www.ijcaip.com/archives/IJCAIP-11-paper1.html [Accessed 30 July 2013].

Brown, A. L. (1992), 'Design Experiments: Theoretical and Methodological Challenges in Creating Complex Interventions', *The Journal of the Learning Sciences*, 2: 141–78.

Bruner, J. (1990), *Acts of Meaning*. Cambridge: Harvard University Press.

Butler-Kisber, L. (2002), 'Artful Portrayals in Qualitative Inquiry: The Road to Found Poetry and Beyond', *Alberta Journal of Educational Research*, 48(3): 229–39.

Cahill, H. (2006), 'Research Acts: Using the Drama Workshop as a Site for Conducting Participatory Action Research', *NJ: Drama Australia Journal*, 30(2): 61–72.

Carr, W. and Kemmis, S. (2003), *Becoming Critical: Education Knowledge and Action Research*. London: Routledge.

Castán Broto, V., Gislason, M. and Ehlers, M. H. (2009), 'Practising Interdisciplinarity in the Interplay Between Disciplines: Experiences of Established Researchers', *Environmental Science and Policy*, 12: 922–33.

Cheng, Y. C. and Tam, M. (1997), 'Multi-Models of Quality in Education', *Quality Assurance in Education*, 5(1): 22–31.

COAG (2011), *National Partnership Agreement on Improving Teacher Quality*. Performance Report for 2011. Canberra: Australian Government. http://www.coagreformcouncil.gov.au/reports [Accessed 30 April 2013].

Cochran-Smith, M. and Donnell, K. (2006), 'Practitioner Inquiry: Blurring the Boundaries of Research and Practice', in J. Green, G. Camilli and P. B. Elmore (eds), *Handbook of Complementary Methods in Education Research*. Mahwah, NJ: Lawrence Erlbaum.

Cochran-Smith, M. and Lytle, S. L. (1999), 'The Teacher Research Movement: A Decade Later', *Educational Researcher*, 28(7): 15–25.

Collins, A. (1992), 'Toward a Design Science of Education', in E. Scanlon and T. O'Shea (eds), *New Directions in Educational Technology*. Berlin: Springer.

Conrad, D. (2004), 'Exploring Risky Youth Experiences: Popular Theatre as a Participatory, Performative Research Method', *International Journal of Qualitative Methods*, 3(1): 12–25.

Costa, A. and Kallick, B. (1993), 'Through the Lens of a Critical Friend', *Educational Leadership*, 51(2): 49–55.

Creswell, J. W. (1994), *Research Design: Qualitative and Quantitative Approaches*. Thousand Oaks, CA: Sage.

Deasy, R. E. (2002), *Critical Links: Learning in the Arts and Student Academic and Social Development*. Arts Education Partnership. http://www.gpo.gov/fdsys/pkg/ERIC-ED466413/pdf/ERIC-ED466413.pdf [Accessed 16 May 2013].

Denzin, N. (2011), 'The Politics of Evidence', in N. Denzin and Y. Lincoln (eds), *The Sage Handbook of Qualitative Research*. Thousand Oaks: Sage.

Denzin, N. and Lincoln, Y. (1994), 'Introduction: Entering the Field of Qualitative Research', in N. Denzin and Y. Lincoln (eds), *Handbook of Qualitative Research*. Thousand Oaks, CA: Sage.

DEST (2012), http://www.dest.gov.au [Accessed 18 July 2013].

Dewey, J. (1897), 'My Pedagogy Creed', *School Journal*, 54: 77–80.

Dewey, J. (1910), *How We Think*. Boston: D.C Heath and Co. Publishers.

Dewey, J. (1937), *Experience and Education*. New York: Macmillan.

Donald, P., Grosling, S., Hamilton, J., Hawkes, N., McKenzie, D. and Stronach, I. (1995), 'No Problem Here: Action Research Against Racism in a Mainly White Area', *British Educational Research Journal*, 21(3): 263–75.

Donelan, K. and O'Brien, A. (2006), 'Walking in Both Worlds: Snuff Puppets at Barak Indigenous College', *Applied Theatre Researcher /IDEA Journal* 7, 1–14.

Eisner, E. (1978), 'Humanistic Trends and the Curriculum Field', *Journal of Curriculum Studies*, 10(3): 97–204.

Elkington, J. (1997), *Cannibals with Forks: The Triple Bottom Line of 21st Century Business*. Oxford: Capstone.

Elmore, R. F. (1996), 'Getting to Scale with Good Educational Practice', *Harvard Educational Review*, 66: 1–16.

ESRC (2012), http://www.esrc.ac.uk/funding-and-guidance/collaboration/knowledge-exchange/opportunities/KT-partnerships.aspx [Accessed 18 July 2013].

Fels, L. (2011), 'A Dead Man's Sweater: Performative Inquiry Embodied and Recognised', in S. Shonmann (ed.), *Key Concepts in Theatre/Drama Education*. Rotterdam: Sense Publishers.

Fels, L. and Belliveau, G. A. (2008), *Exploring Curriculum: Performative Inquiry, Role Drama, and Learning*. Vancouver: Pacific Educational Press.

Fiske, E. (ed.) (1999), *Champions of Change: The Impact of the Arts on Learning*. Washington, DC: The Arts Education Partnership and The President's Committee on the Arts and the Humanities.

Ford Foundation (2012), http://www.fordfoundation.org/issues/educational-opportunity-and-scholarship [Last accessed 18 July 2013].

Freebody, K. (2009), Opportunity Structures and the Drama Classroom: Socioeconomic Status as Topic and Resource. PhD, The University of Melbourne.

Freebody, K., Freebody, P. and Maney, B. (2011), 'School-Society Relations: Projected Communities and the Here-and-Now in Rapidly Changing Times', in D. Bottrell and S. Goodwin (eds), *Schools, Communities and Social Inclusion*. Melbourne: Palgrave Macmillan.

Freebody, P. (2003), *Qualitative Research in Education: Interaction and Practice*. London: Sage.

Freebody, P. and Freebody, K. (2010), *Teachers Researching Communities: A Review of the Research Literature*. Review submitted to Priority Schools Programs, Department of Education and Training NSW.

Freebody, P. and Freebody, K. (2012a), *Teachers Researching Communities: The Case Summaries*. Report submitted to Priority Schools Programs, Department of Education and Training NSW.

Freebody, P. and Freebody, K. (2012b), *Teachers Researching Communities: Community Inquiry Framework*. Report submitted to Priority Schools Programs, Department of Education and Training NSW.

Freebody, P., Freebody, K. and Maney, B. (2011), *Teachers Researching Communities: Final Report*. Report submitted to Priority Schools Programs, Department of Education and Training NSW.

Freire, P. (1970), *The Pedagogy of the Oppressed*. Harmondsworth: Penguin.

Freire, P. (1972), *Cultural Action for Freedom*. Cambridge: Harvard Educational Review.

Gallagher, K. (2007), *The Theatre of Urban: Youth and Schooling in Dangerous Times*. Toronto and Buffalo: University of Toronto Press.

Gallagher, K. (2008), 'The Art of Methodology: A Collaborative Science', in K. Gallagher (ed.), *The Methodological Dilemma: Creative, Critical and Collaborative Approaches to Qualitative Research*. Oxford: Routledge.

Gallagher, K. (2011), 'Theatre as Methodology or, What Experimentation Affords Us', in S. Shonmann (ed.), *Key Concepts in Theatre/Drama Education*. Rotterdam: Sense Publishers.

Goswami, P. and Stillman, P. (1987), *Reclaiming the Classroom: Teacher Research as an Agency for Change*. Upper Montclair, NJ: Boynton/Cook.

Grady, S. (1996), 'Toward the Practice of Theory in Practice', in P. Taylor (ed.), *Researching Drama and Arts Education: Paradigms and Possibilities*. London: Falmer Press.

Griffiths, M. and Woolf, F. (2009), 'The Nottingham Apprenticeship Model: Schools in Partnership with Artists and Creative Practitioners', *British Educational Research Journal*, 35(4): 557–74.

Groundswater-Smith, S. and Irwin, J. (2011), 'Action Research in Education and Social Work', in L. Markauskaite, P. Freebody and J. Irwin (eds), *Methodological Choice and Design: Scholarship, Policy and Practice in Social and Educational Research*. New York: Springer.

Hargreaves, D. H. (1999), 'Revitalising Educational Research: Lessons from the Past and Proposals for the Future', *Cambridge Journal of Education*, 29(2): 239–49.

Hayes, D. (2010), 'Creating a New Learning Program Involves a Number of Distinct Challenges', http://pathingtheway.blogspot.com.au/2010/05/creating-new-learning-program-involves.html [Last accessed 18 July 2013].

Hayes, D. (2011), 'Reconnecting Marginalised Youth to Learning: Reassembling Local Discourses of Schooling and Community Engagement', in D. Bottrell and S. Goodwin (eds), *Schools, Communities and Social Inclusion*. South Yarra: Palgrave Macmillan.

Hayes, D. (2012), 'Re-engaging Marginalised Young People in Learning: The Contribution of Informal Learning and Community-Based Collaborations', *Journal of Education Policy*, 27(5): 641–53.

Heathcote, D. (1984), 'Signs and Portents', in L. Johnson and C. O'Neill (eds.), *Dorothy Heathcote: Collected Writing on Education and Drama*. Evanston, IL: Northwestern University Press.

Heisenberg, W. (1955), 'The Development of the Interpretation of Quantum Theory', in W. Pauli, L. Rosenfeld and V. Weisskopf (eds), *Niels Bohr and the Development of Physics*. New York: McGraw-Hill.

Henry, M. (2000), 'Drama's Ways of Learning', *Research in Drama Education*, 5(1): 45–62.

Hetland, L. and Winner, E. (2001), 'The Arts and Academic Achievement: What the Evidence Shows', *Arts Education Policy Review*, 102(5): 3–6.

Howe, M. and Eisenhart, K. (1990), 'Standards of Qualitative (and Quantitative) Research: A Prolegomenon', *Educational Researcher*, 19(4): 2–9.

Hoy, W. (2010), *Quantitative Research in Education: A Primer*. Thousand Oaks, CA: Sage.

Hughes, J., MacNamara, C. and Kidd, J. (2011), 'The Usefulness of Mess: Artistry, Improvisation and Decomposition in the Practice of Research in Applied

Theatre', in B. Kershaw and H. Nicholson (eds), *Research Methods in Theatre and Performance*. Edinburgh: Edinburgh University Press.

Hunter, L. A. and Leahey, E. (2008), 'Collaborative Research in Sociology: Trends and Contributing Factors', *The American Sociologist*, 39(4): 290–306.

Hurston, Z. N. (1996), *Dust Tracks on a Road*. New York: HarperCollins. (Originally published in 1942).

Jackson, A. Y. and Mazzei, L. A. (eds) (2009), *Voice in Qualitative Inquiry: Challenging Conventional, Interpretive, and Critical Conceptions in Qualitative Research*. London: Routledge.

Janesick, V. (1994), 'The Dance of Qualitative Research Design: Metaphor, Methodolatry and Meaning', in N. Denzin and Y. Lincoln (eds), *Handbook of Qualitative Research*. Thousand Oaks, CA: Sage.

Jeanneret, N. and Brown, R. (2012), 'ArtPlay: Behind the Bright Orange Door', Melbourne Graduate School of Education, http://education.unimelb.edu.au/data/assets/pdf_file/0004/720688/behindtheBrightOrangeDoorARC.pdf [Accessed 19 July 2013].

Kemmis, S. and McTaggart, R. (2005), 'Participatory Action Research', in N. Denzin and Y. Lincoln (eds), *The Sage Handbook of Qualitative Research*, 3rd edn. Thousand Oaks, CA: Sage.

Kettley, N. (2010), *Theory Building in Educational Research*. London and New York, Continuum International Publishing Group.

Kincheloe, J. (2003), *Teachers as Researchers: Qualitative Inquiry as a Path to Empowerment*, 2nd edn. London: Routledge Falmer.

Kincheloe, J. (2008), *Critical Pedagogy Primer*. New York: Peter Lang Publishing.

Klein, J. T. (1996), *Crossing Boundaries: Knowledge, Disciplinarities, and Interdisciplinarities*. Charlottesville and London: University Press of Virginia.

Korthagen, F. A. J. and Kessels, J. P. A. (1999), 'Linking Theory and Practice: Changing the Pedagogy of Teacher Education', *Educational Researcher*, 28(4): 4–17.

Lafreniere, D., Cox, S., Belliveau, G. and Lea, G. W. (2013), 'Performing the Human Subject: Arts-based Knowledge Dissemination in Health Research', *Journal of Applied Arts and Health*, 3(3): 243–57.

Lea, G. W., Belliveau, G., Wager, A. and Beck, J. L. (2011), 'A Loud Silence: Working with Research-Based Theatre and A/R/Tography', *International Journal of Education and the Arts*, 12(6): 1–18.

Ledgard, A. (2007), 'Visiting Time and Boychild: Site-Specific Pedagogical Experiments on the Boundaries of Theatre and Science', http://www.wellcome.ac.uk/stellent/groups/corporatesite/@msh_peda/documents/web_document/wtx050363.pdf [Accessed 12 October 2011].

McCarthy, K. F., Ondaatje, E. H., et al. (2004), *Gifts of the Muse*. Santa Monica, RAND Corporation.

McIntyre, D. (2005), 'Bridging the Gap Between Research and Practice', *Cambridge Journal of Education*, 35(3): 357–82.

MacNamara, C. and Rooke, A. (2007), 'The Pedagogy and Performance of Sci:Dentities', in *Creative Encounters: New Conversations in Science, Education and the Arts*. London: Welcome Trust.

Martin, A. J., Anderson, M. and Adams, R. J. (2012), 'What Determines Young People's Engagement with Performing Arts Events?', *Leisure Sciences*, 34(4): 314–31.

Mitchell, J., Hayes, D. and Mills, M. (2010), 'Crossing School and University Boundaries to Reshape Professional Learning and Research Practices', *Professional Development in Education*, 36(3): 491–509.

Munns, G., Sawyer, W. and Cole, B. (eds) (2013), *Exemplary Teachers of Students in Poverty*. London: Routledge.

Munns, G., Zammit, K. and Woodward, H. (2008), 'Reflections from the Riot Zone: The Fair Go Project and Student Engagement in a Besieged Community', *Journal of Children and Poverty*, 14(2): 157–71.

Newby, E. (2010), *Research Methods for Education*. London: Pearson.

Neylon, T. (2012), 'Life After Elsevier: Making Open Access to Scientific Knowledge a Reality', *The Guardian*, 24 April 2012. http://www.guardian.co.uk [Accessed 1 May 2013].

Nicholson, H. (2005), *Applied Drama: The Gift of Theatre*. Basingstoke, UK: Palgrave Macmillan.

Nieto, S. (2013), 'The Way it Was, the Way it Is', in T. M. Kress and R. Lake (eds), *We Saved the Best for You*. Rotterdam: Sense Publishers.

Nixon, J. and Wellington, J. (2005), ' "Good Books": Is there a Future for Academic Writing within the Educational Publishing Industry?', *British Journal of Sociology of Education*, 26(1): 91–103.

Norris, J. (2009), *Playbuilding as Qualitative Research: A Participatory Arts-Based Approach*. Walnut Creek, CA: Left Coast Press.

OED (2013), Oxford University Press. http://www.oed.com/view/Entry/138320?re directedFrom=partnership [Accessed 18 July 2013].

O'Neill, C. (1995), *Drama Worlds: A Framework for Process Drama*. Portsmouth, NH: Heinemann.

O'Toole, J. and Beckett, D. (2009), *Educational Research: Creative Thinking and Doing*. Oxford: Oxford University Press.

Orfali, A. (2004), *Artists Working in Partnerships with Schools: Quality Indicators and Advice for Planning, Commissioning and Delivery*. UK: Arts Council England.

Park, C. (2006), *The End of the Secret Garden: Reframing Postgraduate Supervision*. http://www.lancs.ac.uk/celt/celtweb/files/ChrisPark.pdf [Accessed 16 May 2013].

Pontecorvo, C. (2007), 'On the Conditions for Generative Collaboration: Learning through Collaborative Research', *Integrative Psychological and Behavioral Science*, 41(2): 178–86.

Prendergast, M. and Saxton, J. (eds) (2009), *Applied Theatre: International Case Studies and Challenges for Practice*. Bristol: Intellect.

Prentki, T. and Preston, S. (2009), 'Applied Theatre: An Introduction', in T. Prentki and S. Preston (eds), *The Applied Theatre Reader*. Abingdon: Routledge.

Punch, M. (1994), 'Politics and Ethics in Qualitative Research', in N. Denzin and Y. Lincoln (eds), *Handbook of Qualitative Research*. Sage: California.

Resilience Research Centre (2013), Resilience Research Centre Home Page. http://www.resilienceproject.org/component/content/article/42-front-page-articles/162-the-resilience-research-centre [Accessed on 30 July 2013].

Reimann, P. (2011), 'Design-Based Research', in Markauskaite, L., Freebody, P. and Irwin, J. (eds), *Methodological Choice and Design: Scholarship, Policy and Practice in Social and Educational Research*. New York: Springer.

Richardson, L. (1994), 'Writing: A Method of Inquiry', in N. Denzin and Y. Lincoln (eds), *Handbook of Qualitative Research*. California: Sage.

Schegloff, E. (2007), *Sequence Organisation in Interaction: A Primer in Conversation Analysis Volume 1*. Cambridge: Cambridge University Press.

Schwandt, T. (2001), *Dictionary of Qualitative Inquiry*, 2nd edn. London: Sage.

Senge, P. (2000), *Schools that Learn*. London: Nicholas Brealey.

Shulman, J. (1990), 'Now You See them, Now You Don't: Anonymity Versus Visibility in Case Studies of Teachers', *Educational Researcher*, 19: 11–16.

Silverman, D. (2000), *Doing Qualitative Research: A Practical Handbook*. London: Sage.

Stevenson, N. (1997), 'Globalization, National Cultures and Cultural Citizenship', *The Sociological Quaterly*, 38(1): 41–66.

Stevenson, N. (2003), 'Cultural Citizenship in the "Cultural" Society: A Cosmopolitan Approach', *Citizenship Studies*, 7(3): 331–48.

Stinson, M. (2009), 'Drama is Like Reversing Everything: Intervention Research as Teacher Professional Development', *RIDE: The Journal of Applied Theatre and Performance*, 14(2): 223–41.

Stinson, M. (2012), 'Accessing Traditional Tales: The Legend of Bukit Merah', in J. Winston (ed.), *Second Language Learning through Drama: Practical Techniques and Applications*. London and New York: Routledge.

Stinson, M. and Freebody, K. (2004), *Drama and Oral Language: Technical Report*. Singapore: Centre for Research in Pedagogy and Practice, National Institute of Education.

Stinson, M. and Freebody, K. (2006), 'Modulating the Mosaic: Drama and Oral Language', in L. McCammon and D. McLauchlan (eds), *Universal Mosaic of Drama and Theatre: The IDEA04 Dialogues*. Ottawa: IDEA Publications.

Stinson, M. and Freebody, K. (2009), 'The Contribution of Process Drama to Improved Results in English Oral Communication', in R. Silver, C. C. M. Goh and L. Alsagoff (eds), *Acquisition and Development in New English Contexts: Evidence from Singapore*. London: Continuum.

von Stump, S., Hell, B. and Chamorro-Premuzic, T. (2011), 'The Hungry Mind: Intellectual Curiosity Is the Third Pillar of Academic Performance', *Perspectives on Psychological Science*, 6(6): 574–88.

Thompson, J. (2006), *Applied Theatre: Bewilderment and Beyond*. Bern: Peter Lang.

Ungar (2013), Pathways to Resilience project. http://resilienceresearch.org/research-and-evaluation/projects/149 [Accessed 18 July 2013].

Vallerand, R. J., Fortier, M. S., and Guay, F. (1997), 'Self-Determination and Persistence in a Real-Life Setting: Toward a Motivational Model of High-School Drop Out', *Journal of Personality and Social Psychology*, 72: 1161–76.

Vallerand, R. J., Paquet, Y., Philippe, F. L. and Charest, J. (2010), 'On the Role of Passion for Work in Burnout: A Process Model', *Journal of Personality*, 78(1): 289–312.

Vygotsky, L. (1978), *Mind in Society*. Cambridge, MA: Harvard University Press.

Wang, F. and Hannafin, M. J. (2005), 'Design-Based Research and Technology-Enhanced Learning Environments', *Educational Technology Research and Development*, 53(4): 5–23.

Wenger, E. (1998), 'Communities of Practice: Learning as a Social System', *Systems Thinker*. http://www.co-i-l.com/coil/knowledge-garden/cop/lss.shtml [Last accessed 18 July 2013].

Whitehead, A. N. (1967), *The Aims of Education and Other Essays*. New York: Free Press. (Originally published in 1929.)

Wyn, J. and White, R. (1997), *Rethinking Youth*. St. Leonards, NSW: Allen and Unwin.

Yarbrough, D. B., Shulha, L. M., Hopson, R. K. and Caruthers, F. A. (2011), *The Program Evaluation Standards: A Guide for Evaluators and Evaluation Users*, 3rd edn. Thousand Oaks, CA: Sage.

Yates, L. (2004), *What does Good Education Research Look Like?* Maidenhead, UK: Open University Press.

Zittoun, T., Baucal, A., Cornish, F. and Gillespie, A. (2007), 'Collaborative Research, Knowledge and Emergence', *Integrative Psychological and Behavioral Science*, 41(2): 208–17.

INDEX

Page numbers in **bold** denote tables and in *italic* denote figures.